Wise Men Talking Series

GUAN ZI
管子说 Says

蔡希勤 编注

□ 责任编辑 陆瑜
□ 翻译 薛彧威
□ 绘图 李士伋

老人家说系列丛书

华语教学出版社
SINOLINGUA

First Edition 2012

ISBN 978-7-5138-0144-7
Copyright 2012 by Sinolingua
Published by Sinolingua
24 Baiwanzhuang Road, Beijing 100037, China
Tel: (86)10- 68320585   68997826
Fax: (86)10- 68997826   68326333
http://www.sinolingua.com.cn
E-mail: hyjx@sinolingua.com.cn
Printed by Beijing Songyuan Printing Co., Ltd.

Printed in the People's Republic of China

老人家 说
Wise Men Talking

俗曰:"不听老人言,吃亏在眼前。"

老人家走的路多,吃的饭多,看的书多,经的事多,享的福多,受的罪多,可谓见多识广,有丰富的生活经验,老人家说的话多是经验之谈,后生小子不可不听也。

在中国历史上,春秋战国时期是中国古代思想高度发展的时期,那个时候诸子并起,百家争鸣,出现了很多"子"字辈的老人家,他们有道家、儒家、墨家、名家、法家、兵家、阴阳家,多不胜数,车载斗量,一时星河灿烂。

后来各家各派的代表曾先后聚集于齐国稷下学官。齐宣王是个开明的诸侯王,因纳无盐丑女钟离春为后而名声大噪。他对各国来讲学的专家学者不问来路一律管吃管住,给予政府津贴。对愿留下来做官的,授之以客卿,造巨室,付万钟;对不愿做官的,也给予"不治事而议论"之特殊待遇。果然这些人各为其主,各为其派,百家争鸣,百花齐放,设坛辩论,著书立说:有的说仁,有的说义,有的说无为,有的说逍遥,有的说非攻,有的说谋攻,有的说性善,有的说性恶,有的说亲非亲,有的说马非马,知彼知己,仁者无敌……留下了很多光辉灿烂的学术经典。

可惜好景不长,秦始皇时丞相李斯递话说"焚书坑儒",结果除秦记、医药、卜筮、种树书外,民间所藏诗、书及百家典籍均被一把火烧个精光。到西汉武帝时,董仲舒又上书提出"罢黜百家,独尊儒术",从此,儒学成了正统,"黄老、刑名百家之言"成为邪说。

"有德者必有言",儒学以外的各家各派虽屡被扫荡,却不断变换着生存方式以求不灭,并为我们保存下了十分丰富的经典著作。在这些经典里,先哲们留下了很多充满智慧和哲理的、至今仍然熠熠发光的至理名言,我们将这些各家各派的老人家的"金玉良言"编辑成这套《老人家说》丛书,加以注释并译成英文,采取汉英对照方式出版,以飨海内外有心有意于中国传统文化的广大读者。

As the saying goes, "If an old dog barks, he gives counsel. "

Old men, who walk more roads, eat more rice, read more books, have more experiences, enjoy more happiness, and endure more sufferings, are experienced and knowledgeable, with rich life experience. Thus, what they say is mostly wise counsel, and young people should listen to them.

The Spring and Autumn (770–476 BC) and Warring States (475–221 BC) periods of Chinese history were a golden age for ancient Chinese thought. In those periods, various schools of thought, together with many sages whose names bore the honorific suffix "Zi," emerged and contended, including the Taoist school, Confucian school, Mohist school, school of Logicians, Legalist school, Military school and Yin-Yang school. Numerous and well known, these schools of thought were as brilliant as the Milky Way.

Later representatives of these schools of thought flocked to the Jixia Academy of the State of Qi. Duke Xuan of Qi was an enlightened ruler, famous for making an ugly but brilliant woman his wife. The duke provided board and lodging, as well as government subsidies for experts and scholars coming to give lectures, and never inquired about their backgrounds. For those willing to hold official positions, the duke appointed them guest officials, built mansions for them and paid them high salaries. Those unwilling to take up official posts were kept on as advisors. This was an era when "one hundred schools of thought contended and a hundred flowers blossomed." The scholars debated in forums, and wrote books to expound their doctrines: Some preached benevolence; some, righteousness; some, inaction; some, absolute freedom; some, aversion to offensive war; some, attack by stratagem; some, the goodness of man's nature; some, the evil nature of man. Some said that relatives were not relatives; some said that horses were not horses; some urged the importance of knowing oneself and one's enemy; some said that benevolence knew no enemy . . . . And they left behind many splendid classic works of scholarship.

Unfortunately, this situation did not last long. When Qin Shihuang (reigned 221-210 BC) united all the states of China, and ruled as the First Emperor, his prime minister, Li Si, ordered that all books except those on medicine, fortune telling and tree planting be burned. So, all poetry collections and the classics of the various schools of thought were destroyed. Emperor Wu (reigned 140-88 BC) of the Western Han Dynasty made Confucianism the orthodox doctrine of the state, while other schools of thought, including the Taoist and Legalist schools, were deemed heretical.

These other schools, however, managed to survive, and an abundance of their classical works have been handed down to us. These classical works contain many wise sayings and profound insights into philosophical theory which are still worthy of study today. We have compiled these nuggets of wisdom uttered by old men of the various ancient schools of thought into this series Wise Men Talking, and added explanatory notes and English translation for the benefit of both Chinese and overseas readers fond of traditional Chinese culture.

目录
CONTENTS

1

不为不可成，不求不可得〔10〕

Never pursue a goal which is unreachable; never seek something that is unattainable.

不远道里，故能威绝域之民〔12〕

Making unexpected military moves in spite of a long distance, so that a far off enemy may behold one's army in awe.

不重之结，虽固必解〔14〕

A casual friendship will fall apart sooner or later despite its temporary firmness.

C

仓廪实则知礼节，衣食足则知荣辱〔16〕

When the granaries are full, men appreciate rites and obligations; when food and clothing are enough, men have a sense of honor and humility.

沉于乐者洽于忧，厚于味者薄于行〔18〕

Indulging in pleasures will bring about misery; coveting delicacies will weaken self-cultivation.

成功立事，必顺于理义〔20〕

Reason and justice are decisive in achieving success.

城郭沟渠不足以固守〔22〕

City walls and moats are not adequate to create a stronghold of

2

defense.

D

大德至仁，则操国得众〔24〕

He who is of virtue and benevolence may be entrusted with the important task of leading the country.

丹青在山，民知而取之〔26〕

When there is cinnabar in mountain stones, people know and mine it.

道者，一人用之，不闻有余〔28〕

It has never been heard that rules and principles are in abundance when applied to an individual.

德厚而位卑者谓之过〔30〕

It's a mistake when a man of solid morality is undervalued.

地大国富，人众兵强，此霸王之本也〔32〕

A vast landmass, big population, and a strong army, which are the bases of a nation's hegemony ...

地辟而国贫者，舟舆饰，台榭广也〔34〕

If the cultivated land doesn't bring prosperity, it means that the financial resources are being spent on luxurious transport and grand buildings.

多忠少欲，智也，为人臣者之广道也〔36〕

Having more honesty and less greed, as a wise man has, is the right way for a faithful official to be.

F

法出于礼，礼出于治〔38〕

Law comes from etiquette, etiquette originates from reason.

法简而易行，刑审而不犯〔40〕

Simple laws facilitate execution, whereas prudent execution prevents crime.

凡兵有大论，必先论其器，论其士〔42〕

Several matters should be discussed before fighting a war, including whether the weapons are sharp, the soldiers are brave ...

凡国之亡也，以其长者也〔44〕

A nation collapses because it is too powerful and prosperous.

凡言之不可复，行之不可再者，有国者之大禁也〔46〕

A wise and able king will not recant his own words, nor do any deed that will bring harm to his people.

G

高山仰之，不可极也。深渊度之，不可测也〔48〕

Towering mountains and deep waters are beyond measurement.

规矩者，方圆之正也〔50〕

Compass and carpenters's square are appliances to rectify circulars and squares.

国虽富，不侈泰，不纵欲〔52〕

A powerful and prosperous nation cannot stand for extravagance and indulgence, nor allow itself to satiate its unchecked desires.

国有宝，有器，有用〔54〕

A country is possessed of treasures, instruments and values.

国有四维〔56〕

Propriety, justice, honesty, and humility are the basis of a nation.

J

计必先定，而出兵于竟〔58〕

Strategy should be made before sending troops abroad to fight a war.

济于舟者，和于水矣。义于人者，祥其神矣〔60〕

Quiet water floats a boat, as harmonious social relations bring good luck and happiness.

近者示之以忠信，远者示之以礼仪〔62〕

Fellow countrymen are treated with honesty and foreigners with etiquette.

君之所审者三〔64〕

There are three principles for the emperor to use to examine officials . . .

厉士利械，则涉难而不匮〔66〕

With brave soldiers and fine weapons, an army will not be exhausted in dangerous situations.

立政出令用人道〔68〕

Government policies should win the support of people.

凌山阬不待钩梯，历水谷不须舟楫〔70〕

Climbing a mountain without a hook ladder, crossing a river without a boat . . .

令重于宝，社稷先于亲戚〔72〕

Decrees outweigh monarchical power, national interests take precedence over family matters.

禄赏加于无功，则民轻其禄赏〔74〕

If rewards are given to idle men, the common people will despise these rewards.

论材量能，谋德而举之，上之道也〔76〕

A monarch is to choose and evaluate the capable men, and then assign them to posts if they are moral.

明君不以禄爵私所爱，忠臣不诬能以干爵禄〔78〕

A wise and able monarch will not practice favoritism, and a loyal official will not cheat for promotion.

明赏不费,明刑不暴,赏罚明则德之至者也〔80〕

Transparent rewards should not be costly, and transparent punishments should not be inhumane. To openly reward and punish is to be of the highest moral standard ...

明主有过, 则反之于身〔82〕

When something malevolent befalls a state, a capable and virtuous monarch will blame and examine himself.

目贵明, 耳贵聪, 心贵智〔84〕

Eyes are to see clearly, ears to hear accurately and the mind to think wisely.

Q

其君子上中正而下谄谀〔86〕

One who has a noble character upholds integrity and despises flattery.

求必欲得, 禁必欲止, 令必欲行〔88〕

It is certain that the pursuit of something is to gain it, a prohibition to prevent something happening, and a decree made in the expectation of it being carried out effectively.

取于民有度, 用之有止, 国虽小必安〔90〕

A moderate expropriation and use of the peoples' means will

bring stability to a small country.

R

日月不明，天不易也〔92〕
A cloudy and foggy day makes both the sun and the moon look dim.

S

山林虽广，草木虽美，禁发必有时〔94〕
Abundance of forest and vastness of grassland does not grant the right to unlimited exploitation.

善者之为兵也，使敌若据虚，若搏景〔96〕
An army comes and goes without a trace under the leadership of a good commander.

上好勇则民轻死〔98〕
The people are unlikely to value their lives when their monarch has warlike propensities.

上妄予则功臣怨〔100〕
Rewards given to idle officials will result in the resentment of the people who have genuinely rendered great service ...

上无固植，下有疑心〔102〕
Officials will be oversensitive and vacillating if the monarch isn't resolute and steadfast.

上下不和，虽安必危〔104〕

If there is no harmony between the high and the low, a safe nation shall be in danger.

少而习焉，其心安焉，不见异物而迁焉〔106〕

From a young age a boy starts to study, and he will thus be constant in his pursuit and immune to various temptations.

身立而民化，德正而官治〔108〕

When a monarch is self-disciplined, the people are cultivated; when a monarch is upright and just, officials are responsible.

审其所好恶，则其长短可知也〔110〕

You can learn someone's merits and failings by looking carefully at their likes and dislikes.

生栋覆屋，怨怒不及〔112〕

The house, built using wet rude lumber, falls as a result of its subsequent structural weaknesses. As such, the builder dare not blame others for his own mistakes.

省刑罚，薄赋敛，则民富矣〔114〕

A reduction in penalties and taxation will bring affluence to the people.

圣人若天然，无私覆也；若地然，无私载也〔116〕

The saint embraces all things unselfishly like the heaven, and bears all things like unselfishly the earth.

圣人上德而下功，尊道而贱物〔118〕

The saint honors ethics and despises fame and wealth, values
moral cultivation and ignores creature comforts.

失天之度，虽满必涸〔120〕

If the laws of heaven are contradicted, anything rich and
abundant can disappear.

收天下之豪杰，有天下之骏雄，故举之如飞鸟〔122〕

The army, assembling heroic men and well-bred horses, raises
troops with the spry lightness of a flying bird.

授事以能，则人上功〔124〕

Assigning a capable person to a post ensures success.

数战则士罢，数胜则君骄〔126〕

The soldiers must be tired of constant war, and the monarch
must be conceited after multiple victories.

所谓德者，先之之谓也〔128〕

The virtuous will show kindness to people at the first opportunity.

T

天不变其常，地不易其则〔130〕

The law of heaven will never change; the earth prospers under
its rule.

天道之极，远者自亲〔132〕

Strangers will establish a harmony among themselves if the law of nature is followed well.

天时不祥，则有水旱〔134〕

When the meteorological pattern is irregular, floods and droughts occur.

天下不患无臣，患无君以使之〔136〕

There is no lack of capable officials, just the want of a monarch to make good use of them.

天下无私爱也，无私憎也〔138〕

The rule of nature is just and disinterested, without partiality and prejudice.

天下者，无常乱，无常治〔140〕

The land under heaven will never be in constant chaos or in everlasting order.

听之术，曰：勿望而距，勿望而许〔142〕

The way to take advice is to examine it after listening to someone; one should not accept or reject it hastily.

W

万物之于人也，无私近也，无私远也〔144〕

Nothing in the world is in shortage or in abundance.

为人君者中正而无私，为人臣者忠信而不党〔146〕

The monarch should be upright and unselfish, an official honest and fair-minded.

我有善则立誉我，我有过则立毁我〔148〕

I was acclaimed after I committed an act of beneficence, and condemned soon after I committed an act of malevolence.

乌集之交，初虽相驩，后必相咄〔150〕

Relations developed in a motley crowd may be intimate at first, but will finally cease to exist.

无土而欲富者忧，无德而欲王者危〔152〕

A man who has no land, yet wants to be rich, is sad; a man who has no virtue, yet wants to be king, is dangerous.

X

贤人不至谓之蔽，忠臣不用谓之塞〔154〕

The capable man is absent because there is someone to dissuade him, the loyal official is ignored because there are obstructions.

宪律制度必法道，号令必著明，赏罚必信密〔156〕

Laws and regulations must follow the principles of the Tao; orders must be clear; rewards and punishments must be appropriate.

小谨者不大立，訾食者不肥体〔158〕

An overcautious person seldom has lofty aspirations, as a man suffering from anorexia cannot gain weight.

孝弟者，仁之祖也〔160〕

Filial piety is the origin of benevolence.

邪莫如蚤禁之〔162〕

It is better to put an end to evil thoughts and deeds in their gestational period.

邪行亡乎体，违言不存口，静然定生，圣也〔164〕

The man who leads a peaceful life, free of desires, and without committing or uttering improper deeds and words, is a saint.

心有欲者，物过而目不见，声至而耳不闻也〔166〕

A greedy man cannot see or hear clearly.

信之者仁也，不可欺者智也〔168〕

Honesty and credit are benevolence. And a wise man will not be cheated.

刑罚不足以畏其意〔170〕

Punishments cannot change the will of the common people.

形不正者德不来〔172〕

A person with a wretched appearance must be evil inside.

Y

言是而不能立，言非而不能废〔174〕

If the good person is cast aside while the evil one stays in office ...

一年之计，莫如树谷〔176〕

When planning for a year, plant cereals.

一期之师，十年之蓄积殚〔178〕

A troop of soldiers fighting a war will cost ten years of national savings.

有善者不留其赏，故民不私其利〔180〕

If good conduct is rewarded immediately, the people will not pursue personal interests.

欲王天下而失天之道，天下不可得而王也〔182〕

To unite the land of heaven without following the laws of heaven is impossible.

Z

早知敌而独行，有蓄积则久而不匮〔184〕

There is no war that cannot be won if an army knows much about its enemy in advance; it will not be exhausted because financial and material supply is guaranteed.

朝忘其事，夕失其功〔186〕

One who has accomplished nothing at the end of the day must not have worked hard during the day.

召远在修近，闭祸在除怨〔188〕

If one gets along well with the people around him, those who live afar will wish to go to him for shelter. If resentment is appeased,

14

turmoil will not arise.

政之所兴，在顺民心〔190〕

A government decree that meets the aspirations of the common people will be implemented effectively.

治国有三器〔192〕

There are three instruments—order, weapons, and salary—needed to govern a nation effectively.

治国之道，必先富民〔194〕

Enriching the people is the prerequisite way to administrate a nation.

众若时雨，寡若飘风〔196〕

To besiege the enemies and lure them into surrender when overwhelming in number; to launch a surprise attack and triumph over the enemies when few in number.

壮者无怠，老者无偷〔198〕

Be neither slothful in the meridian of one's life, nor drift along in one's old age.

追亡逐遁若飘风，击刺若雷电〔200〕

An army should chase the fleeing enemies as quickly as the wind, and attack the enemies as fiercely as a thunderbolt.

管子说

GUAN ZI SAYS

　　管子，姓管名夷吾，字仲。春秋齐国人，初事公子纠，及公子小白（桓公）即位，公子纠死，管仲被囚在鲁国。鲁大夫施伯对鲁侯说："管仲者，天下之贤人也，大器也。在楚，则楚得意于天下，在晋，则晋得意于天下。"鲍叔向齐桓公推荐管仲说："君且欲霸王，非管夷吾不可。"于是管仲执齐国之政，通货积财，富国强兵，九合诸侯，一匡天下，使桓公成为春秋五霸之首，皆管仲之谋也。

　　管仲为政齐国，善因祸而为福，转败而为功。主张"仓廪实则知礼节，衣食足则知荣辱，上服度则六亲固"。管仲死后，"齐国遵其政，常强于诸侯"。孔子曰："微管仲，吾其被发左衽矣！"

　　Guan Zi's name was Guan Yiwu, with the courtesy name Zhong. He was a native of the State of Qi in the Spring and Autumn Period. He initially served Prince Jiu, who died after Prince Xiaobai（Qi Huangong）ascended to the throne. Afterwards, Guan Zhong was jailed in the State of Lu. Shi Bo, a senior official of the state said to the Duke of Lu: "Guan Zhong is a person of intelligence and integrity, and is a very talented man. Whichever state has him will surely establish itself as a great power." Guan Zhong's bosom friend Bao Shu, a senior official of Qi also recommended him to Qi Huangong: "Should Your Majesty wish to rule over the empire, none other than Guan Yiwu can help you to achieve this aim." Thus, Guan Zhong subsequently took charge of the state affairs of Qi by developing trade and accumulating wealth, and enriching the country and strengthening its military forces. All of this contributed greatly to making Huangong the first and most prominent of the Five Overlords of the Spring and Autumn Period.

When in charge of the affairs of Qi, Guan Zhong was adept at benefiting from adversity and converting defeats into victories. He believed that "when the granaries are full, men appreciate rites and obligations; when food and clothing are enough, men have a sense of honor and humility, and when people in power observe rites and abide by the law, their relatives will be on harmonious terms". After his death, the State of Qi continued following his policies, and thus maintained their dominance among the several states for a long span of time. Confucius once said: "Without Guan Zhong, we would have remained barbarian tribes and never become civilized. "

必得之事不足赖也，必诺之言不足信也

An easily obtained post is easy to lose; a casually made promise is not worth relying upon.

管子说

必得之事不足赖也，必诺之言不足信也。

《管子·形势》

An easily obtained post is easy to lose; a casually made promise is not worth relying upon.

【注释】

必得之事：小人以不正当手段得到的职务。《管子·形势解》："圣人之求事也，先论其理义，计其可否。故义则求之，不义则止。可则求之，不可则止。故其所得事者，常为身宝。小人之求事也，不论其理义，不计其可否。不义亦求之，不可亦求之。故其所得事者，未尝为赖也。故曰：必得之事，不足赖也。"事，职务。《论语·卫灵公》："事君敬其事而后其食。"《韩非子·五蠹》："无功而受事，无爵而显荣。"**赖**：依靠，凭借。《尚书·大禹谟》："六府三事允治，万世永赖。"又《吕刑》："一人有庆，兆民赖之。"**诺**：应允。《老子》第63章："轻诺必寡信，多易必多难。"

【译文】

随便得到的职务靠不住，随便许下的诺言不足信。

不明于象，而欲论材审用，犹绝长以为短

To select capable people without knowing their characters is like blindly making long things short . . .

不明于象，而欲论材审用，犹绝长以为短，续短以为长。

《管子·七法》

To select capable people without knowing their characters is like blindly making long things short and short things long, which is to act against the laws of nature.

【注释】

象：凡形于外者皆曰象，如气象，星象。《易·系辞上》："在天成象，在地成形，变化见矣。"**绝长以为短，续短以为长**：注曰："鹤胫非所断，凫胫非所续也。"胫，脚胫。《庄子·骈拇》："长者不为有余，短者不为不足。是故凫胫虽短，续之则忧；鹤胫虽长，断之则悲。故性长非所断，性短非所续，无所去忧也。"

【译文】

不知道形象变化，而想选拔贤才使用，就好像天下万物可以随心所欲地截长为短、续短为长一样。

不明于则，而欲出号令，犹立朝
夕于运均之上

To issue orders without understanding the laws and regulations is just like erecting a sundial upon a pottery wheel . . .

不明于则，而欲出号令，犹立朝夕于运均之上。

《管子·七法》

To issue orders without understanding the laws and regulations is just like erecting a sundial upon a pottery wheel, using which you can never distinguish east from west.

【注释】

则：法则。《诗经·大雅·烝民》："天生烝民，有物有则。"朝夕：即日晷，古代用日影以测量时间的仪器。运均：唐·尹知章注曰："均，陶者之轮。立朝夕所以正东西也。"《墨子·非命上》："言必立仪，言而毋仪，譬犹运钧之上而立朝夕者也。"如果把日晷（朝夕）立在转轮之上是无法辨别东西方向的。

【译文】

不明白事物变化的法则，却要发号命令，就好比把日晷立在制作陶器的转轮之上，是无法辨别东西方向的。

不为爱人枉其法，故曰法爱于人

The king will never pervert the law owing to personal preference. Ultimately, the law is more important than personal feeling.

管子说

不为爱人枉其法，故曰法爱于
人。不为重禄爵分其威，故曰威重于
爵禄。

《管子·七法》

The king will never pervert the law owing to personal preference. Ultimately, the law is more important than personal feelings. The monarch's authority should never be diffused by the assignment of government posts, because eventually authority weighs more than position.

【注释】

法爱于人：注曰："法者，崇替所由，故弃所爱而存其法。"存法之心甚于爱人之情。威重于爵禄：注曰："威者，人君以服海内，必不得已，宁散爵禄，不可分威也。"君主的尊严重于官职的分配。

【译文】

不因私人感情而枉法，所以说法重于情。不因官职的分配而分散君主的权威，所以说君主的权威重于官职的分配。

不为不可成，不求不可得

Never pursue a goal which is unreachable; never seek something that is unattainable.

不为不可成，不求不可得，不处不可久，不行不可复。

《管子·牧民》

Never pursue a goal which is unreachable; never seek something that is unattainable. Never be content with temporary ease and comfort, and never tyrannize and humiliate the people.

【注释】

管子曰："不为不可成者，量民力也。不求不可得者，不强民以其所恶也。不处不可久者，不偷取世也。不行不可复者，不欺民也。"复：唐·房玄龄注曰："重也。欺民之事，不可重行也。"

【译文】

不做办不到的事，不求得不到的东西，不偷生苟安，不干欺民之事。

不远道里，故能威绝域之民

Making unexpected military moves in spite of a long distance, so that a far off enemy may behold one's army in awe.

不远道里，故能威绝域之民。不险山河，故能服恃固之国。独行无敌，故能令行禁止。

《管子·七法》

Making unexpected military moves in spite of a long distance, so that a far off enemy may behold one's army in awe; being valiant and skilful in battle without heavily depending on geographical advantages, so that the defenses of any enemy, no matter how formidable, may be shattered. This is the way in which an invincible military leader may issue orders and not meet with any hindrance to their victory.

【注释】

绝域：极远的地域。《西京杂记》："傅介子年十四，好学书，尝弃觚叹曰：'大丈夫当立功绝域，何能坐事散儒！'"恃：凭借。《晋书·张载传》："兴实由德，险亦难恃。"独行：《管子·七法》："有雷电之战，故能独行而无敌矣。"注曰："雷电，天之威怒，故莫敢为敌。敌人望风自追，故曰独行也。"

【译文】

出奇兵不怕路程遥远，所以能威震远方之敌。英勇善战不怕山川险峻，所以能威服凭借险阻固守的敌国。无人敢对抗的军队，所以能有令则行有禁则止。

不重之结，虽固必解

A casual friendship will fall apart sooner or later despite its temporary firmness.

不重之结，虽固必解。道之用也，贵其重也。

《管子·形势》

A casual friendship will fall apart sooner or later despite its temporary firmness; the key to the art of making friends lies in seriousness.

【注释】

管子曰："圣人之与人约结也，上观其事君也，内观其事亲也，必有可知之理，然后约结。约结而不袭于理，后必相倍。"重：庄重。《论语·学而》："君子不重则不威，学则不固。"解：分裂。《史记·张耳陈馀传》："今独王陈，恐天下解也。"

【译文】

随随便便的交情，虽一时稳固后必分裂。交友之道的应用，关键在于庄重。

仓廪实则知礼节，衣食足则知荣辱

When the granaries are full, men appreciate rites and obligations; when food and clothing are enough, men have a sense of honor and humility.

仓廪实则知礼节，衣食足则知荣辱，上服度则六亲固，四维张则君令行。

《管子·牧民》

When the granaries are full, men appreciate rites and obligations; when food and clothing are enough, men have a sense of honor and humility; when people in power observe rites and abide by the law, their relatives will be on harmonious terms, and when the "four cardinal traditional virtues" of propriety, justice, honesty and humility are upheld, orders issued by the monarch will proceed without hindrance.

【注释】

仓廪（lǐn）：储藏粮食的仓库。《荀子·王制》："并聚之于仓廪。"《礼记·月令》季春之月："命有司发仓廪。"疏："谷藏曰仓，米藏曰廪。"荣辱：荣耀和耻辱。《荀子·荣辱》："先义而后利者荣，先利而后义者辱。"服度：遵礼守法。六亲：六亲所指各说不同。《老子》："六亲不和有孝慈。"王弼注云："父母兄弟妻子也。"四维：礼义廉耻。《管子·牧民》："四维不张，国乃灭亡。"

【译文】

先使民富足然后教以礼仪，吃饱穿暖再讲荣耀和耻辱。执政者遵礼守法，六亲和睦相处，倡导礼义廉耻，号令才能通行无阻。

沉于乐者洽于忧，厚于味者薄于行

Indulging in pleasures will bring about misery; coveting delicacies will weaken self-cultivation.

沉于乐者洽于忧，厚于味者薄于行，慢于朝者缓于政，害于国家者危于社稷。

《管子·中匡》

Indulging in pleasures will bring about misery; coveting delicacies will weaken self-cultivation; neglecting the imperial court will loosen the reins of government affairs, and lacerating the country will jeopardize state power.

【注释】

齐桓公设酒宴招待管子"公执爵，夫人执尊，觞三行，管仲趋出"。桓公很不高兴，于是管仲说了上面的话。**沉于乐者洽于忧**：注曰："乐过则忧博"。沉，溺于所好。《尚书·胤征》："沈乱于酒，畔官离次。"沈，同"沉"。洽，沾润。《尚书·大禹谟》："好生之德，洽于民心。"疏："洽谓沾渍优渥。洽于民心，言润泽多也。"**厚**：与"薄"相反。《庄子·养生主》："彼节者有间，而刀刃者无厚。"**朝**：朝廷，帝王受朝议事之处。《孟子·梁惠王上》："使天下仕者皆欲立于王之朝。"引申为政事。

【译文】

沉溺于享乐会带来忧患，贪图美味就会放松行为修养，怠慢于朝廷就会放松对政事的处理，伤害了国家就会危及政权。

成功立事，必顺于理义

Reason and justice are decisive in achieving success.

成功立事，必顺于理义，故不理不胜天下，不义不胜人。

《管子·七法》

Reason and justice are decisive in achieving success. Therefore, by conforming with reason, the country will be conquered; by conforming with justice, the people will be conquered, and vice versa.

【注释】

立事：建立事业，立经国之事。《汉书·刑法志》："《书》曰：'立功立事，可以永年。'言为政而宜于民者，功成事立，则受天禄而永年命。"理义：道理与正义。《孟子·告子上》："故理义之悦我心，犹刍豢之悦我口。"理，道理，法则。《易·系辞上》："易简而天下之理得矣。"《礼记·仲尼燕居》："礼也者，理也。"疏："理，谓道理，言礼者使万物合于道理也。"义，宜，适宜。合理、适宜的事称义。《易·乾》："利物足以和义。"

【译文】

事业成功一定要合于理义，所以不合于理就不能战胜天下，不合于义就不能战胜别人。

城郭沟渠不足以固守

City walls and moats are not adequate to create a stronghold of defense.

城郭沟渠不足以固守，兵甲强力不足以应敌，博地多财不足以有众，唯有道者能备患于未形也，故祸不萌。

《管子·牧民》

City walls and moats are not adequate to create a stronghold of defense; powerful troops have not enough capabilities to succeed when faced with a formidable enemy; vast lands and abundant wealth do not always lead to an increased population. It is only those who uphold justice that can provide against future strife.

【注释】

城郭：内城与外城，泛指城邑。《管子·度地》："内为之城，外为之郭。"《孟子·公孙丑下》："三里之城，七里之郭。"沟渠：城壕，壕沟。《礼记·礼运》："城郭沟池以为固。"《荀子·议兵》："城郭不办，沟池不拊。"不足：不够。《商君书·算地》："今世主有地方数千里，食不足以待役实仓，而兵为邻敌，臣固为世主患之。"兵甲：武器军备。未形：没有显露出来。萌：发端。《战国策·赵策二》："愚者暗于成事，智者见于未萌。"

【译文】

仅靠城郭壕沟还不能牢固防守，仅靠兵力强盛还不能应对强敌，地广财多也不能增加百姓人数，只有得道之人才能防患于未然，祸患才不会发生。

大德至仁，则操国得众

He who is of virtue and benevolence may be entrusted with the important task of leading the country.

大德至仁，则操国得众；见贤能让，则大臣和同；罚不避亲贵，则威行于邻敌。

《管子·立政》

He who is of virtue and benevolence may be entrusted with the important task of leading the country; he who stands aside in favor of one more qualified will cause cabinet officials to unify and work with one heart; and he who gives punishment without the exception of royal kin may be endowed with military power.

【注释】

管子曰："君之所慎者四：一曰大德不至仁，不可以授国柄。二曰见贤不能让，不可与尊位。三曰罚避亲贵，不可使主兵。四曰不好本事，不务地利而轻赋敛，不可与都邑。此四务者，安危之本也。"和同：和睦同心。《左传·成公十六年》："民生敦庞，和同以听。"《管子·五辅》："上下交引而不和同，故处不安而动不威。"亲贵：王室至亲。《晋书·武帝纪》："平吴之后，天下乂安，遂怠于政术，耽于游宴，宠爱后党，亲贵当权，旧臣不得专任。"邻敌：与我为敌的邻国。《荀子·议兵》："故兵大齐则制天下，小齐则制邻敌。"

【译文】

能行仁德之政，可以担当治国重任。能尊贤礼让，大臣间才能和睦同心。刑罚不避亲贵，可以掌握兵权。

丹青在山，民知而取之

When there is cinnabar in mountain stones, people
know and mine it.

丹青在山，民知而取之。美珠在渊，民知而取之。是以我有过为，而民毋过命。

《管子·小称》

When there is cinnabar in mountain stones, people know and mine it; when there are precious pearls in deep water, people know and obtain them; and when I commit an error, people will know and point it out unerringly.

【注释】

丹青在山，民知而取之。美珠在渊，民知而取之：注曰："丹青与珠，各有可用之性，故虽在山泉而藏，人犹知而取之，况在于人怀善而不知乎。"丹青，丹砂和青䨼，两种可制颜料的矿石。美珠，宝珠。是以我有过为，而民毋过命：注曰："我身有过为，人必知而名之，无有过而妄命者也。"过为，错误的行为。过命，妄命。

【译文】

山石中有丹青，老百姓知道取而用之。深水中有宝珠，老百姓知道取而用之。我有过错，老百姓一定会知道，不会说错的。

道者，一人用之，不闻有余

It has never been heard that rules and principles are in abundance when applied to an individual.

道者，一人用之，不闻有余；天
下行之，不闻不足。此谓道矣。

《管子·白心》

It has never been heard that rules and principles are in abundance when applied to an individual; it is also unheard of that they are adequate as all obey and carry them forward. There is no telling as to how much or little rules and principles are.

【注释】

道：规律，事理。《易·说卦》："是以立天之道曰阴与阳，立地之道曰柔与刚，立人之道曰仁与义。"《庄子·养生主》："庖丁释刀对曰：臣之所好者道也，进乎技矣。"唐·房玄龄注曰："多少皆足者道也。"道是空虚无形的，故无"有余"、"不足"之说。

【译文】

道用于一人，没听说有余剩；天下人遵道而行，没听说道不够用。无多无少这就是道。

德厚而位卑者谓之过

It's a mistake when a man of solid morality is under-valued.

德厚而位卑者谓之过，德薄而位尊者谓之失。宁过于君子，而毋失于小人。过于君子，其为怨浅；失于小人，其为祸深。

《管子·立政》

It's a mistake when a man of solid morality is undervalued, or a man of weak morality is overvalued, in officialdom. It is better to have a man of noble character take a low position than to offer a man with a mean disposition a high post, as the latter will only bring benign discontent, while the former will lead to malignant disaster.

【注释】

德厚：德高。厚，与"薄"相反。《庄子·养生主》："彼节者有间，而刀刃者无厚。"过：过失。《尚书·大禹谟》："宥过无大，刑故无小。"失：错误。《礼记·学记》："教也者，长善而救其失者也。"

【译文】

德厚但职位低叫做"过"，德薄而处尊位叫做"失"。宁肯让君子职位低，也不要让小人处尊位。君子职位低，其受埋怨事小；小人处尊位，那可就祸害深远了。

地大国富，人众兵强，此霸王之本也

A vast landmass, big population, and a strong army, which are the bases of a nation's hegemony...

地大国富，人众兵强，此霸王之
本也，然而与危亡为邻矣。

《管子·重令》

A vast landmass, big population, and a strong army,
which are the bases of a nation's hegemony, are also beto-
kens of its approaching collapse.

【注释】

管子曰："天道之数，人心之变。天道之数，至则反，盛则衰。人心之变，有余
则骄，骄则缓怠。夫骄者骄诸侯，骄诸侯者，诸侯失于外。缓怠者，民乱于内。诸
侯失于外，民乱于内，天道也，此危亡之时也。"邻：近。《管子·水地》："邻以理
者，知也。"注："邻，近也。"

【译文】

土地广博，国家富裕。人口众多，兵力强盛。这是
称霸的资本，然而也是国家临近危亡的时候。

地辟而国贫者，舟舆饰，台榭广也

If the cultivated land doesn't bring prosperity, it means that the financial resources are being spent on luxurious transport and grand buildings.

管子说

地辟而国贫者，舟舆饰，台榭广也。赏罚信而兵弱者，轻用众，使民劳也。

《管子·权修》

If the cultivated land doesn't bring prosperity, it means that the financial resources are being spent on luxurious transport and grand buildings. If clear rewards and punishments can't ensure a strong army, it proves that human resources are being imprudently and excessively used.

【注释】

管子曰："舟车台榭广，则赋敛厚矣。轻用众，使民劳，则民力竭矣。赋敛厚则下怨上矣，民力竭则令不行矣。下怨上，令不行，而求敌之勿谋己，不可得也。" **辟**：开拓。《诗经·大雅·江汉》："式辟四方，彻我疆土。" **信**：的确。《左传·昭公元年》："子晳信美矣。" **轻**：轻率，轻易。《老子》第63章："夫轻诺必寡信。"

【译文】

土地已开辟而国家仍然贫穷，是因为把财力都用在了豪华车船和楼堂馆所的建设上。赏罚分明而国家兵力薄弱，是因为轻率使用民力使百姓劳累不堪。

多忠少欲，智也，为人臣者之广
道也

Having more honesty and less greed, as a wise man
has, is the right way for a faithful official to be.

多忠少欲，智也，为人臣者之广道也。

《管子·枢言》

Having more honesty and less greed, as a wise man has, is the right way for a faithful official to be.

【注释】

忠：忠诚。《论语·学而》："为人谋而不忠乎？"《荀子·大略》："比干子胥忠而君不用。"欲：贪欲。物欲、情欲、色欲。《老子》第19章："见素抱朴，少私寡欲。"智：知道，认识。通"知"。《墨子·经说下》："夫名，所以明正所不智，不以所不智疑所明。"广道：大道，正道。

【译文】

忠诚寡欲，是明智的表现，也是为人臣之正道。

法出于礼，礼出于治

Law comes from etiquette, etiquette originates from reason.

法出于礼，礼出于治。治、礼，道也。万物待治、礼而后定。

《管子·枢言》

Law comes from etiquette, etiquette originates from reason. Etiquette and reason are the Tao, the absolute principle underlying the universe. Nothing will be in disorder if it follows the principles of the Tao.

【注释】

法出于礼：法由礼出。管子曰："人故相憎也。人之心悍，故为之法。"法，法则，法度。《周礼·天官·小宰》："以法掌祭礼、朝觐、会同、宾客之戒具。"注："法，谓其礼法也。"礼，规定社会行为的法则、规范、仪式的总称。《论语·为政》："道之以德，齐之以礼，有耻且格。"《荀子·礼论》："先王恶其乱也，故制礼义以分之。"礼出于治：礼出于理。治，理。《礼记·乐记》："礼也者，理之不可易者也。"理，道理，法则。《易·系辞上》："易简而天下之理得矣。"《礼记·仲尼燕居》："礼也者，理也。"疏："理，谓道理，言礼者使万物合于道理也。"

【译文】

法出于礼仪，礼仪出于道理。道理和礼仪就是道。天下万物合于道后自然安定。

法简而易行，刑审而不犯

Simple laws facilitate execution, whereas prudent execution prevents crime.

法简而易行，刑审而不犯，事约而易从，求寡而易足。

《管子·桓公问》

Simple laws facilitate execution, whereas prudent execution prevents crime. Concise government policies make more people follow the law of the country, and men with less desire feel more content.

【注释】

简：简要。《易·系辞上》："易见易知，简则易从。"《论语·雍也》："居敬而行简，以临其民，不亦可乎。"审：慎重。《韩非子·存韩》："故曰：'兵者，凶器也'，不可不审用也。"约：简单，简略。《荀子·不苟》："（君子）总天下之要，治海内之众，若使一人。故操弥约而事弥大。"

【译文】

法度简要就会便于实行，量刑慎重就不会再去触犯，政事简约就容易听从，要求少了人们就容易满足。

凡兵有大论，必先论其器，论
其士

Several matters should be discussed before fighting a war, including whether the weapons are sharp, the soldiers are brave . . .

凡兵有大论，必先论其器，论其士，论其将，论其主。

《管子·参患》

Several matters should be discussed before fighting a war, including whether the weapons are sharp, the soldiers are brave, the general is resourceful, and whether the king is right in selecting the general.

【注释】

管子曰："器滥恶不利者，以其士予人也。士不可用者，以其将予人也。将不知兵者，以其主予人也。主不积务于兵者，以其国予人也。"《汉书·晁错传》："故《兵法》曰：器械不利，以其卒予敌也；卒不可用，以其将予敌也；将不知兵，以其主予敌也；君不择将，以其国予敌也。四者，兵之至要也。此兵法即指《管子》。论：评论，辩论。《礼记·王制》："凡官民材必先论之，论辩然后使之。"《吕氏春秋·应言》："人与不入之时，不可不熟论也。"注："论，辩也。"

【译文】

凡带兵作战先要论辩，论其武器是否精良，其士卒是否勇敢，其主将是否知兵，其国君选将是否得人。

凡国之亡也，以其长者也

A nation collapses because it is too powerful and prosperous.

凡国之亡也，以其长者也。人之自失也，以其所长者也。故善游者死于梁也，善射者死于中野。

《管子·枢言》

A nation collapses because it is too powerful and prosperous, and a man makes mistake for he is wiser than others. Therefore, those drowned in water are always good swimmers and those killed in the battlefield are often excellent archers.

【注释】

长：善，优。《孟子·公孙丑上》：" '敢问夫子恶乎长？'曰：'我知言，我善养吾浩然之气'。"梁：障水之堤。《庄子·达生》："孔子观于吕梁，县水三千仞，流沫四十里，见一丈夫游之。"中野：荒野之中，也指野战。《墨子·兼爱中》："诸侯不相爱，则必野战。"

【译文】

国家灭亡，往往是因其强盛而好战导致的。人犯错误，往往是因其有过人之长处而骄傲导致的。所以善游泳者死于水，善射者死于战争。

凡言之不可复，行之不可再者，
有国者之大禁也

A wise and able king will not recant his own words, nor do any deed that will bring harm to his people.

凡言之不可复，行之不可再者，有国者之大禁也。

《管子·形势解》

A wise and able king will not recant his own words, nor do any deed that will bring harm to his people.

【注释】

管子曰："言之不可复者，其言不信也。行之不可再者，其行贼暴也。故言而不信则民不附，行而贼暴则天下怨。民不服，天下怨，此灭亡之所生也，故明主禁之。"**言之不可复**："出言而离父子之亲，疏君臣之道，害天下之众，此言之不可复者也，故明主不言也。"**行之不可再**："身行不正，使人暴虐，遇人不信，行发于身而为天下笑者，此不可复之行，故明主不行也。"**有国者**：君主。

【译文】

凡是言而无信的话和行而害民的事，圣明之君是不说不做的。

高山仰之，不可极也。深渊度之，不可测也

Towering mountains and deep waters are beyond measurement.

高山仰之，不可极也。深渊度之，不可测也。神明之德，正静其极也。

《管子·九守》

Towering mountains and deep waters are beyond measurement. Likewise, the combination of virtue and wisdom is boundless and omnipresent.

【注释】

极：穷尽，终了。《诗经·唐风·鸨羽》："悠悠苍天，曷其有极。"**神明之德**：德配神明。注曰："（所听之言）不审察者，常为彼所知，故戒之当如高山深渊，不可极而测之。既如山渊，则其德配神明，而正且静。如此者，其有穷极矣。"

【译文】

山高不见顶，渊深不可测。神明之德，无边无际，无处不在。

规矩者，方圆之正也

Compass and carpenters's square are appliances to rectify circulars and squares.

规矩者，方圆之正也。虽有巧目利手，不如拙规矩之正方圆也。故巧者能生规矩，不能废规矩而正方圆。

《管子·法法》

Compass and carpenters's square are appliances to rectify circulars and squares, which are more valuable than a skilled craftsman. Although it is a skilled craftsman who makes a compass and a carpenter's square, he can not rectify the circular and square without them.

【注释】

管子曰："虽圣人能生法，不能废法而治国。故虽有明智高行，倍法而治，是废规矩而正方圆。"倍法，违背法律。倍，背向。规矩：校正圆形方形之器。《孟子·离娄上》："离娄之明，公输子之巧，不以规矩，不能成方员。"员，同"圆"。拙：笨。与"巧"相对。《老子》第45章："大巧若拙，大辩若讷。"

【译文】

规矩是校正方圆的器具，虽有目明手巧之人，也不如有个笨规矩校正方形圆形。所以巧匠能制造出规矩，却不能不用规矩去校正方圆。

国虽富，不侈泰，不纵欲

A powerful and prosperous nation cannot stand for extravagance and indulgence, nor allow itself to satiate its unchecked desires.

国虽富，不侈泰，不纵欲；兵虽强，不轻侮诸侯，动众用兵，必为天下正理。

《管子·重令》

A powerful and prosperous nation cannot stand for extravagance and indulgence, nor allow itself to satiate its unchecked desires. It must be the principle universally applied that a military power shouldn't bully others at will.

【注释】

侈泰：奢侈放纵。《管子·八观》："俭财用，禁侈泰。"纵欲：尽其所欲，不加克制。《左传·昭公十年》："《书》曰：'欲败度，纵败礼'，我之谓矣。我实纵欲而不能自克也。"理：道理，法则。《易·系辞上》："易简而天下之理得矣。"《礼记·仲尼燕居》："礼也者，理也。"疏："理，谓道理，言礼者使万物合于道理也。"

【译文】

国家虽然富强，也不能奢侈放纵，对欲望不加克制。兵力虽强盛，也不能随便动用武力欺侮别国，这一定会成为天下正道。

国有宝，有器，有用

A country is possessed of treasures, instruments and values.

国有宝，有器，有用。城郭、险阻、蓄藏，宝也。圣智，器也。珠玉，末用也。先王重其宝器而轻其用，故能为天下。

《管子·枢言》

A country is possessed of treasures, instruments and values. By their treasures is meant complete city walls, strong defenses and abundant stores; by instruments, virtue and wisdom; by values, hidden pearls and jewels. The former kings conquered and unified the whole country because in their wisdom they knew that treasures and instruments were far more important than pearls and jewels.

【注释】

有宝：唐·房玄龄注："城郭完，险阻修，则寇盗息。蓄藏积，民无饥，故为宝也。"有器：管子曰："圣智，器也。"注曰："圣无不通，智无遗策，二者可操以成事，故曰器。"圣，无事不通曰圣。有用：管子曰："珠玉，末用也。"注曰："珠玉者，饥不可食，寒不可衣，费多而益少，故为末用也。"末用，商用，并非贱珠玉之价值也。农为本，商为末。

【译文】

国家有宝，有器，有用。城郭完备、防御设施齐全、存粮充足，这些是国家的宝。可以解决国家大事的圣明和智谋，就是国家的器。珠宝美玉居末位，有其商用价值。先王知道宝和器重要，看轻珠玉，所以能统一天下。

国有四维

Propriety, justice, honesty, and humility are the basis of a nation.

国有四维。一维绝则倾，二维绝则危，三维绝则覆，四维绝则灭。倾可正也，危可安也，覆可起也，灭不可复错也。

《管子·牧民》

Propriety, justice, honesty, and humility are the basis of a nation. A lack of propriety leads to an improper society, a shortage of justice puts a nation into chaos, a want of honesty will bring a nation down and an absence of humility will ruin it. An improper society can be improved, chaos quieted, a nation's downfall halted, but there will be no remedy once the nation is in ruins.

【注释】

四维：维，结物的大绳。也象征能使事物固定下来的意识或力量。所以旧时统治者把礼、义、廉、耻称作四维。《管子·牧民》："四维张，君令行。"又"四维不张，国乃灭亡。"绝：灭。危：凶险，不安。《庄子·则阳》："安危相易，祸福相生。"覆：翻，倾倒。

【译文】

立国要靠礼、义、廉、耻四项。失去第一项则国家偏斜，失去第二项则国家混乱，失去第三项则国家倾倒，失去第四项则国家灭亡。偏斜尚可扶正，混乱还可以安定，倾倒还可以扶起，灭亡就不能再建起来了。

计必先定，而兵出于竟

Strategy should be made before sending troops abroad to fight a war.

计必先定，而兵出于竟。计未定
而兵出于竟，则战之自败，攻之自毁
者也。

《管子·参患》

Strategy should be made before sending troops abroad to
fight a war, otherwise the army will be defeated in a confron-
tation and destroyed in an offensive attack.

【注释】

计必先定，而兵出于竟：计谋必先制定，然后出兵。《孙子·计篇》张预注引作
"计先定于内而后兵出境。"计，计数，谋略。《汉书·高帝纪》："用陈平秘计得
出。"竟，疆界。同"境"。《礼记·曲礼上》："入竟而问禁，入国而问俗，入门而
问讳。"

【译文】

计谋必须先制定出来，然后军队才可出境作战。如
果计谋未定就出兵作战，战则自败，攻则自毁。

济于舟者，和于水矣。义于人
者，祥其神矣

Quiet water floats a boat, as harmonious social relations bring good luck and happiness.

济于舟者，和于水矣。义于人
者，祥其神矣。

《管子·白心》

Quiet water floats a boat, as harmonious social relations
bring good luck and happiness.

【注释】

济于舟者，和于水矣：注曰："水和静无有波浪，则能济舟。"济，渡过。《左传·文公三年》："秦伯伐晋，济河焚舟。"和，和顺，谐合。《易·乾》："保合大和。"《礼记·中庸》"发而皆中节谓之和。"**义于人者，祥其神矣**：注曰："与人理相宜，则神与之福祥也。"义，宜。《论语·公冶长》："其养民也惠，其使民也义。"

【译文】

水能载舟在于水平静没有波浪，与人和睦相处的人神灵会保佑他幸福吉祥。

近者示之以忠信，远者示之以礼仪

Fellow countrymen are treated with honesty and foreigners with etiquetle.

近者示之以忠信，远者示之以礼仪。行此数年，而民归之如流水。

《管子·霸形》

If, for a good period of years, fellow countrymen are treated with honesty and foreigners with etiquetle, the people, from afar or nearby, will come like flowing water and pledge their allegiance to the state.

【注释】

示：以事告人，让人看见。《老子》第 36 章："国之利器，不可以示人。"《庄子·应帝王》："尝试与来，以予示之。"释文："示之，本亦作视。"忠信：儒家主张的一种品德。意为言语诚恳实在。《论语·卫灵公》："子张问行。子曰：'主忠信，行笃敬。'"礼仪：行礼之仪式。《诗经·小雅·楚茨》："献酬交错，礼仪卒度。"

【译文】

以诚恳实在对待国内百姓，以礼仪相待他国民众。这样实行若干年后，远近百姓都会像流水一样归附。

君之所審者三

There are three principles for the emperor to use to examine officials . . .

君之所审者三：一曰德不当其位，二曰功不当其禄，三曰能不当其官。此三本者，治乱之原也。

《管子·立政》

There are three principles for the emperor to use to examine officials: First, if their moral standards match their high position. Second, if their contributions are deserving of their salary. Third, if they are equal to their jobs. The law and order of a nation depends on these principles.

【注释】

管子曰："国有德义未明于朝者，则不可加于尊位；功力未见于国者，则不可授与重禄；临事不信于民者，则不可使任大官。"审：慎重。《韩非子·存韩》："故曰：'兵，凶器也'，不可不审用也。"三本：谓治、乱各有三法也。《荀子·礼论》："礼有三本：天地者，生之本也；先祖者，类之本也；君师者，治之本也。"原：水源，根本。《左传·昭公九年》："犹衣服之有冠冕，木水之有本原。"《礼记·孔子闲居》："必达于礼乐之原。"

【译文】

国君对官吏考查有三项：其德义是否能加于尊位，其功劳是否能授与重禄，其才能是否能当大官。这三项是国家或治或乱的根源。

厉士利械，则涉难而不匮

With brave soldiers and fine weapons, an army will not be exhausted in dangerous situations.

厉士利械，则涉难而不匮。进无所疑，退无所匮，敌乃为用。

《管子·兵法》

With brave soldiers and fine weapons, an army will not be exhausted in dangerous situations. Without hesitating to attack or having scruples in retreat, the army will be able to fully contain the enemies.

【注释】

厉士：振奋之士。《管子·七法》："兵弱而士不厉。" 利械：锐利的兵器。械，器物。涉难：进入危险境地。进无所疑，退无所匮：管子曰："教器备利，进退若雷电，而无所疑匮。" 匮，竭也。敌乃为用：注曰："既无疑匮，敌乃服从而为己用。" 敌人被牵着鼻子走。

【译文】

兵士勇敢，武器精良，虽进入危险境地也不会力竭。进攻不犹豫，后退无顾虑，敌人完全听从自己指挥。

立政出令用人道

Government policies should win the support of people.

立政出令用人道，施爵禄用地道，举大事用天道。

《管子·霸言》

Government policies should win the support of people, government officials should be justly appointed, and the great undertaking should follow the order of nature.

【注释】

立政出令用人道：注曰："政令须合人心。"立政，推行政事。人道，人类社会道德规范。《易·系辞下》："有天道焉，有人道焉。"这里人道指人和。**施爵禄用地道**：注曰："地道平而无私。"施爵禄，给官员爵位与俸禄。地道，地利。**举大事用天道**：注曰："心应天时，然后可以举大事。"天道，天时。

【译文】

推行政事要符合人心，使用官员要公平无私，每行大事要应天时。

凌山阬不待钩梯，历水谷不须舟楫

Climbing a mountain without a hook ladder, crossing a river without a boat...

凌山阬不待钩梯，历水谷不须舟楫，径于绝地，攻于恃固，独出独入，而莫之能止。

《管子·兵法》

Climbing a mountain without a hook ladder, crossing a river without a boat, the army men penetrate the desolate land, attacking the enemies who take the difficulty of access as a defense; they come and go as freely as entering an uninhabited land, all resistance is broken.

【注释】

凌：登，逾越。汉·张衡《东京赋》："然后凌天地，绝飞梁。"阬（gāng）：丘陵，土冈。历：涉水。《诗经·邶风·匏有苦叶》："深则厉，浅则揭。"连衣涉水称厉，同"厉"，提起衣服涉水称揭。径：同"经"。

【译文】

登山不用钩梯，渡水不用舟楫，过孤绝之地，攻击恃险固守之敌，独来独往，如入无人之境，没有人能阻挡。

令重于宝，社稷先于亲戚

Decrees outweigh monarchical power, national interests take precedence over family matters.

令重于宝，社稷先于亲戚，法重于民，威权贵于爵禄。

《管子·法法》

Decrees outweigh monarchical power, national interests take precedence over family matters, laws outweigh public opinions, and authority should not be defused while offering nobility and salary to those who make contributions to society.

【注释】

管子曰："令者，人主之大宝也。""故不为重宝轻号令，不为亲戚后社稷，不为爱民枉法律，不为爵禄分威权。"令：号令，命令。《诗经·齐风·东方未明》："倒之颠之，自公令之。"社稷：本指土、谷之神，后作为国家政权的标志。《孟子·尽心下》："民为贵，社稷次之，君为轻。"威权：威势权力。《汉书·杜周传》附杜钦："威权泰盛而不忠信，非所以安国家也。"爵禄：爵位和俸禄。《荀子·性恶》："妻子具而孝衰于亲，嗜欲得而信衰于友，爵禄盈而忠衰于君。"

【译文】

法令重于君主的权力，国家利益重于亲戚的利益，法律重于民意，威势权力比爵位俸禄更重要。

禄赏加于无功，则民轻其禄赏

If rewards are given to idle men, the common people will despise these rewards.

禄赏加于无功，则民轻其禄赏；民轻其禄赏，则上无以劝民；上无以劝民，则令不行矣。

《管子·权修》

If rewards are given to idle men, the common people will despise these rewards; if the common people despise these rewards, the ranking officials will lose the means to motivate the common people; if the ranking officials fail to motivate the common people, government decrees will cease to be effective.

【注释】

禄赏：以俸禄对有功者赏赐。劝：勉励，奖励。《论语·为政》："举善而教不能则劝。"《左传·成公十四年》："惩恶而劝善。"

【译文】

用俸禄奖赏无功人员，百姓就会轻视这种奖赏；百姓轻视这种奖赏，执政者就没有了勉励百姓的手段；执政者没有勉励百姓的手段，政令就不能通达。

论材量能，谋德而举之，上之道也

A monarch is to choose and evaluate the capable men, and then assign them to posts if they are moral.

论材量能，谋德而举之，上之道也。专意一心，守职而不劳，下之事也。

《管子·君臣上》

A monarch is to choose and evaluate the capable men, and then assign them to posts if they are moral. An official is to be loyal and devoted, and fulfill his duties faithfully and uncomplainingly.

【注释】

论材量能：选择有才华的人。论（lùn），选择。《国语·齐语》："权节其用，论比协材。"注："论，择也。"量（liàng），衡量。《荀子·君道》："论德而定次，量能而授官。"谋德而举之：注曰："谋知其德，然后举用之。"谋，图谋，营求。《论语·卫灵公》："君子谋道不谋食。"守职而不劳：注曰："不以职事为劳苦。"

【译文】

选择有才华的人，知其有德，然后举用，这是国君之道。专心一意，任劳任怨，这是臣下之事。

明君不以禄爵私所爱，忠臣不诬能以干爵禄

A wise and able monarch will not practice favoritism, and a loyal official will not cheat for promotion.

明君不以禄爵私所爱，忠臣不诬能以干爵禄。

《管子·法法》

A wise and able monarch will not practice favoritism, and a loyal official will not cheat for promotion.

【注释】

管子曰："君不私国，臣不诬能，行此道者，虽未大治，正民之经也。"注曰："治虽未大，足成正民之经。"**明君不以禄爵私所爱**：唐·房玄龄注曰："贤明之君，必公诚于国，以一其民人之心。"私，凡属一己者皆曰私。对"公"而言。《尚书·周官》："以公灭私，民其允怀。"爱，亲爱的人。《韩非子·主道》："诚有过，则虽近爱必诛。"**忠臣不诬能以干爵禄**：唐·房玄龄注曰："忠臣必直道而求进。"诬，欺骗。《韩非子·显学》："无参验而必之者，愚也；弗能必而据之者，诬也。故明据先王，必定尧舜者，非愚则诬也。"

【译文】

贤明之君不用官位俸禄徇私情，忠于君主的臣子不用欺骗手段谋取官职。

明赏不费，明刑不暴，赏罚明则
德之至者也

Transparent rewards should not be costly, and transparent punishments should not be inhumane. To openly reward and punish is to be of the highest moral standard ...

管子说

明赏不费，明刑不暴，赏罚明则德之至者也，故先王贵明。

《管子·枢言》

Transparent rewards should not be costly, and transparent punishments should not be inhumane. To openly reward and punish is to be of the highest moral standard, that is why the late emperor valued transparency in political life.

【注释】

明：显示，公开。《易·系辞下》："因贰以济民行，以明失得之报。"《墨子·旗帜》："建旗其暑，令皆明白知之，曰某子旗。"费：用财多。《论语·尧曰》："君子惠而不费。"又："因民之所利而利之，斯不亦惠而不费乎？"暴：凶恶。《易·系辞上》："上慢下暴，盗思伐之矣。"

【译文】

公开赏赐不会被认为用财多，公开刑罚不会被认为凶暴，赏罚公开是最高的道德，所以先王重视政治透明。

明主有过，则反之于身

When something malevolent befalls a state, a capable and virtuous monarch will blame and examine himself.

明主有过，则反之于身；有善，则归之于民。有过而反之身，则身惧。有善而归之民，则民喜。

《管子·小称》

When something malevolent befalls a state, a capable and virtuous monarch will blame and examine himself; when something benevolent appears, he will give the credit to the common people. Mistakes lead to self-examination, so he will attach great importance to self-cultivation for fear of committing improper acts. The common people will feel joyful and valued if they are credited with doing good deeds for the state.

【注释】

反之于身：反过来要求自己。《易·蹇》："君子以反身修德。"也作"反躬"。《礼记·乐记》："不能反躬，天理灭矣。"反求诸身是儒家一种重要的修养方法，指通过反省来检验自己的思想和行为是否符合道德标准。有过而反之身，则身惧：注曰："过反于身，则惧而修德也。"

【译文】

圣明君主有过错，会反躬自省；有善行，会归之于百姓。有过错时懂得反省，就会因害怕有错而更加注意自身修养。有善行归之于百姓，百姓就会得善而欢喜。

目贵明，耳贵聪，心贵智

Eyes are to see clearly, ears to hear accurately and the mind to think wisely.

目贵明，耳贵聪，心贵智。以天下之目视，则无不见也。以天下之耳听，则无不闻也。以天下之心虑，则无不知也。辐凑并进，则明不塞矣。

《管子·九守》

Eyes are to see clearly, ears to hear accurately and the mind to think wisely properly. (A saint) Looking through the eyes of the people, there is nothing that cannot be seen; listening with the ears of the people, there is nothing that cannot be heard; thinking with the mind of the people, there is no task that cannot succeed. If people act with one heart and mind, they can do anything.

【注释】

注曰："言圣人不自用其聪明思虑，而任之天下，故明者为之视，聪者为之听，智者为之谋，辐凑并进，不亦宜乎？故曰：'明不可塞'。"**辐凑**：车辐集中于轴心。喻人或物聚集一处。

【译文】

眼睛重要在于看得明白，耳朵重要在于听得真切，心重要在于思虑得当。（圣人）用天下人的眼睛去看，就没有看不见的事；用天下人的耳朵去听，就没有听不到的声音；用天下人的心去谋划，就没有不成功的。如此万众一心上下通达，就没有办不成的事。

其君子上中正而下谄谀

One who has a noble character upholds integrity and despises flattery.

其君子上中正而下谄谀，其士民贵武勇而贱得利。

《管子·五辅》

One who has a noble character upholds integrity and despises flattery; one who serves in the military values courage and does not act according to personal interests.

【注释】

上：崇尚，提倡。《管子·立政》："上完利。" 中正：正直。屈原《离骚》："耿吾得此中正。" 下：轻视，看不上。谄谀：谄媚，奉承。谄，献媚。《论语·学而》："贫而无谄，富而无骄。" 谀，用不实之词奉承人。《荀子·修身》："以不善先人者谓之谄，以不善和人者谓之谀。" 士民：古代四民中学道艺或习武勇的人。《穀梁传·成公元年》："古者有四民：有士民，有商民，有农民，有工民。" 注："士民，学习道艺者。" 贱得利：尹知章注曰："贱苟得之利也。"

【译文】

君子崇尚正直而鄙视谄谀，士民看重勇武而轻视苟得之利。

求必欲得，禁必欲止，令必欲行

It is certain that the pursuit of something is to gain it, a prohibition to prevent something happening, and a decree made in the expectation of it being carried out effectively.

求必欲得，禁必欲止，令必欲行。求多者其得寡，禁多者其止寡，令多者其行寡。

《管子·法法》

It is certain that the pursuit of something is to gain it, a prohibition to prevent something happening, and a decree made in the expectation of it being carried out effectively. However, greater pursuits result in little gain, too many prohibitions bring about more violations, and additional decrees lead to less compliance.

【注释】

管子曰："求而不得则威日损，禁而不止则刑罚侮，令而不行则下凌上。故未有能多求而多得者也，未有能多禁而多止者也，未有能多令而多行者也。"**求多者其得寡**：唐·房玄龄注曰："无厌则难供，故其得寡。"意谓贪多无厌，不能得到满足。**禁多者其止寡**：注曰："法令滋章，盗贼多有。"**令多者其行寡**：注曰："再三则渎，故其行寡。"

【译文】

追求就一定是想要得到，下禁令就一定是想要禁止，下命令就一定是想要执行。贪求太多得到的反而会少，禁令太多服从的人反而会少，号令太多能执行的反而会少。

取于民有度，用之有止，国虽小
必安

A moderate expropriation and use of the peoples'
means will bring stability to a small country.

取于民有度，用之有止，国虽小必安。取于民无度，用之不止，国虽大必危。

《管子·权修》

A moderate expropriation and use of the peoples' means will bring stability to a small country, while an excessive use of such will send a large nation into crisis.

【注释】

管子曰："地之生财有时，民之用力有倦，而人君之欲无穷。以有时与有倦，养无穷之君，而度量不生于其间，则上下相疾也。"度：限度。《左传·昭公二十年》："征敛无度，宫室日更，淫乐不违。"止：限止。《易·艮》："时止则止，时行则行。"

【译文】

取于民财有限度，用财有限止，国家虽小一定会安定。取于民财无度，用财没有限止，国家虽大必会出现危机。

日月不明，天不易也

A cloudy and foggy day makes both the sun and the moon look dim.

日月不明，天不易也。山高而不见，地不易也。言而不可复者，居不言也。行而不可再者，君不行也。

《管子·形势》

A cloudy and foggy day makes both the sun and the moon look dim. The rugged land keeps the mountains from view. A wise monarch should not promise something out of his reach, or carry out deeds considered unjust.

【注释】

日月不明，天不易也：注曰："日月无不明，假令不明，是天有云气而不易也。""人主犹日月也，群臣多奸立私，以拥蔽主，则主不得昭察其臣下，臣下之情不得上通，故奸邪日多而人主愈蔽。故曰：日月不明，天不易也。"（《管子·形势解》）山高而不见，地不易也：注曰："山高无不见，假令不见，是地多险阻不平易也。""人主犹山也，左右多党比周，以壅其主，则主不得见。故曰：山高而不见，地不易也。"（《管子·形势解》）复：实行，兑现，实践诺言。《论语·学而》："信近于义，言可复也。"

【译文】

日月不明，是因为有云气遮蔽。山高看不见，是因为地面不平有险阻隔挡。不能兑现的话，明主不说。不正当的行为，明主不做。

山林虽广，草木虽美，禁发必有时

Abundance of forest and vastness of grassland does not grant the right to unlimited exploitation.

山林虽广，草木虽美，禁发必有时。国虽充盈，金玉虽多，宫室必有度。

《管子·八观》

Abundance of forest and vastness of grassland does not grant the right to unlimited exploitation; richness in the treasure of a nation does not automatically allow for the construction of an excessively lavish palace.

【注释】

发：生长。《诗经·大雅·生民》："实发实秀。"疏："发者，穗生于苗，初发苗生也。"充盈：丰盛、富足。度：限度。《左传·昭公二十年》："征敛无度，宫室日更，淫乐不违。"《国语·周语》："用物过度妨于财。"

【译文】

山林虽然广阔，草木虽然茂盛，但砍伐一定要有时间限制。国家虽然富裕，金玉宝物虽多，但建造宫室一定要有限度。

善者之为兵也，使敌若据虚，若搏景

An army comes and goes without a trace under the
leadership of a good commander.

善者之为兵也，使敌若据虚，若搏景。

《管子·兵法》

An army comes and goes without a trace under the leadership of a good commander. In this way, the enemy will be unable to locate, catch, or attack them.

【注释】

据虚：抓空。据，抓，拏。《老子》第55章："毒虫无螫，猛兽不据。"搏景：搏击影子，比喻事之无成。景，同"影"。《史记·主父偃传》："夫匈奴之性，兽聚而鸟散，从之如搏影。"《汉书》作"搏景"。

【译文】

善于用兵的人指挥军队，总能来无影，去无踪，使敌人抓不住，打不着，看不见。

上好勇则民轻死

The people are unlikely to value their lives when their monarch has warlike propensities.

上好勇则民轻死，上好仁则民轻财。故上之所好，民必甚焉。

《管子·法法》

The people are unlikely to value their lives when their monarch has warlike propensities, just as they are unlikely to be mean with their money under the rein of one who has strong sense of justice. In such circumstances, the people must cater too much to what the king likes.

【注释】

　　管子曰："凡民从上也，不从口之所言，从情之所好者也。" **轻死**：轻弃生命。**上之所好，民必甚焉**：《墨子·兼爱中》："昔者楚灵王好细腰，灵王之臣，皆以一饭为节，胁息然后带，扶墙然后起。"胁息，吸气。

【译文】

　　君王崇尚武勇，那么百姓就会轻视生命，君王崇尚仁义，那么百姓就会仗义疏财。所以君王喜欢的东西，百姓一定会过分喜欢。

上妄予则功臣怨

Rewards given to idle officials will result in the resentment of the people who have genuinely rendered great service . . .

上妄予则功臣怨，功臣怨而愚民操事于妄作，愚民操事于妄作，则大乱之本也。

《管子·法法》

Rewards given to idle officials will result in the resentment of the people who have genuinely rendered great service, hence making it a hot item among those unreasonable persons, which is the basic source of turmoil.

【注释】

上妄予：管子曰："令未布而民或为之，而赏从之，则是上妄予也。"注曰："未布而为，所谓先时者也。当刑而赏，故曰妄与也。"愚民操事于妄作：不明事理的人就会拿这件事进行炒作。愚，蠢笨，无知。操，持，拿着。妄，非分，越轨。

【译文】

国君乱赏无功之人会使有功之人产生怨恨情绪，功臣怨恨会使不明事理的人拿这件事进行炒作，这是大乱的本原。

上无固植，下有疑心

Officials will be oversensitive and vacillating if the monarch isn't resolute and steadfast.

上无固植，下有疑心。国无常经，民力必竭，数也。

《管子·法法》

It is a general rule that officials will be oversensitive and vacillating if the monarch isn't resolute and steadfast; that manpower will be drained if a nation doesn't have stable long-term policies.

【注释】

固植：坚定的意志。宋玉《招魂》："弱颜固植。"注："植，志也。"疑心：猜测之心。《商君书·更法》："疑行无成，疑事无功。"常经：长期不变的政策。经，法则，原则。《左传·宣公十二年》："兼弱攻昧，武之善经也。"数：唐·房玄龄注曰："数，理也。国无常经，人力必竭，而曰不竭者，此非理之言也。"《韩非子·孤愤》："夫以疏远与近爱信争，其数不胜也。"

【译文】

国君没有坚定的意志，臣下就怀疑不定。国家没有长期不变的政策，役使无度，民力必定枯竭，这是常理。

上下不和，虽安必危

If there is no harmony between the high and the low, a safe nation shall be in danger.

臣不亲其主，百姓不信其吏，上下离而不和，故虽自安必且危之。故曰：上下不和，虽安必危。

《管子·形势解》

A nation will run into crisis if the citizens, don't work together with one ideal and one will, or the officials lack loyalty to the monarch and the trust of the people. Therefore, if there is no harmony between the high and the low, a safe nation shall be in danger.

【注释】

上下不和，虽安必危：唐·房玄龄《管子》注："能持满者，则与天合。能安危者，则与人合。不合于天，虽满必涸。不合于人，虽安必危。"能安危者，指能够使国家安定也能使国家出现危机的人（执政者），关键是他的治政方针是否合于民心。

【译文】

臣下不忠于主上，百姓不相信官吏，上下离心离德，国家虽然安定必会出现危机。所以说：上下不和，虽安必危。

少而习焉，其心安焉，不见异物而迁焉

From a young age a boy starts to study, and he will thus be constant in his pursuit and immune to various temptations.

少而习焉，其心安焉，不见异物而迁焉。

《管子·小匡》

From a young age a boy starts to study, and he will thus be constant in his pursuit and immune to various temptations.

【注释】

习：学。《吕氏春秋·听言》："蜂门始习于甘蝇。"蜂门，古代善射者，即逢蒙。甘蝇，古代传说中的神箭手。逢蒙曾跟他学射。心安：心有寄托，安适无憾。《国语·齐语》："其幼者言悌，少而习焉，其心安焉。"异物：唐·房玄龄注曰："异物，谓异事，非其所当习者。"奇巧的物品谓异物。《尚书·旅獒》："不作无益害有益，功乃成；不贵异物贱用物，民乃足。"

【译文】

少年学习，心思安定，不会见异思迁。

身立而民化，德正而官治

When a monarch is self-disciplined, the people are cultivated; when a monarch is upright and just, officials are responsible.

身立而民化，德正而官治。治官化民，其要在上。

《管子·君臣上》

When a monarch is self-disciplined, the people are cultivated; when a monarch is upright and just, officials are responsible. The cultivation of the people and the responsibility of the officials depend on the conduct of the monarch.

【注释】

身立：立身，树立己身。《孝经·开宗明义》："立身行道，扬名于后世，以显父母，孝之终也。" 民化：化民。《老子》第57章："我无为而民自化，我好静而民自正。" 化，化育。《管子·心术上》："化育万物谓之德。" 德正：正德。端正德行。《尚书·大禹谟》："正德，利用，厚生，惟和。"疏："正德者，自正其德。"

【译文】

君主修养好，百姓就会得到教化，君主德行端正，官吏就能管理好。管好官吏教化百姓，关键在君主。

审其所好恶，则其长短可知也

You can learn someone's merits and failings by looking carefully at their likes and dislikes.

审其所好恶，则其长短可知也；观其交游，则其贤不肖可察也。二者不失，则民能可得而官也。

《管子·权修》

You can learn someone's merits and failings by looking carefully at their likes and dislikes, and measure someone's competency by examining their friends. The person with both a good personality and a high level of competency is qualified for officialdom.

【注释】

好恶（hào wù）：喜爱和厌恶。《诗经·小雅·彤弓》："我有嘉宾，中心好之。"《左传·隐公三年》："周郑交恶。" 长短（cháng duǎn）：优缺点，长处与不足。《孟子·公孙丑上》："敢问夫子恶乎长？"曰："我知言，我善养吾浩然之气。"《新唐书·颜师古传》："每作文章，令指摘疵短。" 二者：谓好恶，交游二事。

【译文】

仔细观察他的好恶，就知道他的长处和不足。审视他交游的对象，就知道他有无才能。如果这两项没问题，就可以做官了。

生栋覆屋，怨怒不及

The house, built using wet rude lumber, falls as a result of its subsequent structural weaknesses. As such, the builder dare not blame others for his own mistake.

生栋覆屋，怨怒不及。弱子下瓦，慈母操箠。

《管子·形势》

The house, built using wet rude lumber, falls as a result of its subsequent structural weaknesses. As such, the builder dare not blame others for his own mistakes. However, a kind mother may get angry and flog the child with a whip only for his breaking of a tile, because it is not the mother herself who makes the mistake.

【注释】

唐·房玄龄《管子》注："言人以生栋造舍，虽至覆屋，但自咎而已，不敢怒及他人。至弱子下瓦，所损不多，慈母便操箠而怒之。喻人主过由己作，虽大而吞声；过发他人，虽小而振怒也。" **生栋覆屋**：用没有干透的新木（未干之木）为栋梁建屋，栋易变形使屋倒塌。比喻咎由自取。生，没有干透和加工的，新的。栋，房屋的正梁。覆，翻掉。《管子·形势解》："栋生桡不胜任，则屋覆而人不怨者，其理然也。" **弱子下瓦，慈母操箠**：《管子·形势解》："弱子，慈母之所爱也，不以其理衍下瓦，则必母咎之。"弱，年少。箠（chuí），鞭打。

【译文】

用没有干透的新木作正梁建屋，结果梁变形而房屋倒塌，因咎由自取而不敢怒及他人。幼子打碎瓦片，慈母就生气地拿鞭子打他，因为过错是他人造成的，虽然错小也引人发怒。

省刑罚，薄赋敛，则民富矣

A reduction in penalties and taxation will bring affluence to the people.

省刑罚，薄赋敛，则民富矣。乡建贤士，使教于国，则民有礼矣。出令不改，则民正矣。此爱民之道也。

《管子·小匡》

A reduction in penalties and taxation will bring affluence to the people, a virtuous man invited to take charge of local education will enlighten the people, and constancy in governmental decrees will ensure the peoples' sense of civic duty. These are the proper ways to love the people.

【注释】

省：节约，减省。《孟子·梁惠王上》："省刑罚，薄税敛。"乡：行政区域单位。所辖范围，历代不同。周制，万二千五百家为乡。春秋齐制，郊内以五家为轨，十轨为里，四里为连，十连为乡；郊外以五家为轨，六轨为邑，十邑为率，十率为乡。正：端正。《国语·周语》："且夫立无陂，正也。"

【译文】

减少刑罚，少收税，老百姓就会富裕。乡建学校请贤良之士负责教育，老百姓就会懂得礼仪。政令不朝令夕改，老百姓就会行为端正。这就是爱民的正道。

圣人若天然，无私覆也；若地然，无私载也

The saint embraces all things unselfishly like the heaven, and bears all things unselfishly like the earth.

圣人若天然，无私覆也；若地然，无私载也。私者，乱天下者也。

《管子·心术下》

The saint embraces all things unselfishly like the heaven, and bears all things unselfishly like the earth. The source of turmoil in the land under heaven is selfish desire.

【注释】

覆：遮盖，掩蔽。《诗经·大雅·生民》："诞寘之寒冰，鸟覆翼之。"《礼记·中庸》："博厚所以载物也，文明所以覆物也。"《老子》第25章："人法地，地法天。"唐·李约《道德真经新注》："法地，如地之无私载；法天，如天之无私覆。"私：私欲。指不正当的个人欲望。《淮南子·说山》："公道不立，私欲得容者，自古及今，未尝闻也。"

【译文】

圣人像天一样无私地笼盖万物；像地一样无私地承载万物。私欲是使天下混乱的根源。

圣人上德而下功，尊道而贱物

The saint honors ethics and despises fame and wealth, values moral cultivation and ignores creature comforts.

圣人上德而下功，尊道而贱物。
道德当身，故不以物惑。

《管子·戒第》

The saint honors ethics and despises fame and wealth, values moral cultivation and ignores creature comforts. With such a sense of morality, one can be immune to material temptations.

【注释】

上德：以德为重。上通"尚"。《左传·僖公二十八年》："原轸将中军，胥臣佐下军，上德也。" 下功：看轻功利。贱物：轻视名利。贱，轻视。《礼记·乐记》："广则容奸，狭则思欲，感条畅之气而灭平和之德，是以君子贱之也。" 物，物欲，谓名利之事。道德当身，故不以物惑：注曰："身苟有道德，岂名利之物能惑哉。"

【译文】

圣人崇尚道德，轻视功利，尊重道德修养，轻视物质享受。身有道德，所以不受物欲迷惑。

失天之度，虽满必涸

If the laws of heaven are contradicted, anything rich and abundant can disappear.

地大国富，民众兵强，此盛满之国也。虽已盛满，无德厚以安之，无度数以治之，则国非其国，而民无其民也。故曰：失天之度，虽满必涸。

《管子·重令》

A wealthy nation vast in territory, large in population and strong in military might is a rich and powerful nation. However, without a proper ethical code and legal system, the nation will decline and fall, and its people will drift away. Thus it is that if the laws of heaven are contradicted, anything rich and abundant can disappear.

【注释】

盛满：富足，充实。德厚：德高。度数：法制。天之度：天道。管子曰："天之道，满而不溢，盛而不衰。明主法象天道，故贵而不骄，富而不奢，行理而不惰，故能长守贵富，久有天下而不失也。"

【译文】

地域辽阔，国家富有，人口众多，军队强大，这是一个强盛的国家。虽然国家强盛，但如果没有道德来安定天下，不用法制来治理国家，那么国家就会衰亡，人民就会流失。所以说：失去天道，虽盈满也一定会干涸。

收天下之豪杰，有天下之骏雄，故
举之如飞鸟

The army, assembling heroic men and well-bred horses, raises troops with the spry lightness of a flying bird.

收天下之豪杰，有天下之骏雄，故举之如飞鸟，动之如雷电，发之如风雨，莫当其前，莫害其后，独出独入，莫敢禁圉。

《管子·七发》

The army, assembling heroic men and well-bred horses, raises troops with the spry lightness of a flying bird, operates with the great momentum of a thunderbolt, marches with the awesome quickness of a storm, and has no barriers before it or troops in pursuit behind it, as the enemies will become terror-stricken on hearing of its coming, and it shall breaks through all resistance like it is entering an uninhabited land.

【注释】

举之如飞鸟：喻轻捷。管子曰："有飞鸟之举，故能不险山河矣。"注曰："轻捷如飞鸟，故不以山河为险。"动之如雷电：以雷霆万钧之势不可挡也。管子曰："有雷电之战，故能独行而无敌矣。"注曰："雷电，天之威怒，故莫敢为敌。"发之如风雨：兵贵神速。管子曰："风雨之行，故能不远道里矣。"注曰："行疾如风雨，故不以道里为远。"圉（yù）：通"御"。

【译文】

集合天下豪杰之士和良马组成军队，起兵轻捷如飞鸟，动之以雷霆万钧之势，行军神速如疾风暴雨，使敌人闻风丧胆，前不敢挡，后不敢追，如入无人之境，敌人不能抵御。

授事以能，则人上功

Assigning a capable person to a post ensures success.

授事以能，则人上功。审刑当罪，则人不易讼。

《管子·问第》

Assigning a capable person to a post ensures success. People will not dispute against one another because there already have existed reasonable punishments.

【注释】

管子曰："凡立朝廷，问有本纪。爵授有德，则大臣兴义。"**授事以能，则人上功**：注曰："有能然后得事，故人上功。"事，职务。《论语·卫灵公》："事君敬其事而后其食。"能，才能。《周礼·天官·大宰》："以八统诏王驭万民：一曰亲亲，二曰敬敬，三曰进贤，四曰使能。"**审刑当罪，则人不易讼**：注曰："易，犹交也。所刑皆当其罪，故人不交相讼。"易，交易，交换。《易·系辞下》："交易而退，各得其所。"

【译文】

任用有才能的人，人们就会崇尚建功立业。刑罚得当，所以人不会互相争讼。

数战则士罢，数胜则君骄

The soldiers must be tired of constant war, and the monarch must be conceited after multiple victories.

数战则士罢，数胜则君骄。夫以骄君使罢民，则国安得无危！

《管子·兵法》

The soldiers must be tired of constant war, and the monarch must be conceited after multiple victories. If the conceited monarch tried to command these tired soldiers, how much danger the nation would be in!

【注释】

数：一个以上不确定的数目，几个。《孟子·尽心下》："堂高数仞，榱题数尺。" 罢（pí）：疲困，软弱。《韩非子·说林上》："魏攻中山而弗能取，则魏必罢，罢则魏轻。"

【译文】

连续作战兵士一定疲惫，数次胜利君主必然骄傲。由骄傲的君主指挥疲惫不堪的兵士，国家怎么会没有危险呢！

所谓德者，先之之谓也

The virtuous will show kindness to people at the first opportunity.

所谓德者，先之之谓也。故德莫如先，应适莫如后。

《管子·枢言》

The virtuous will show kindness to people at the first opportunity, however, it is better to gain mastery of a battle by striking only after the enemy has struck.

【注释】

适 (dí)：通"敌"。《礼记·燕义》："君独升立席上，西面特立，莫敢适之义也。"疏："莫敢适，言臣下莫敢与君匹敌。"《史记·范睢传》："攻适伐国。"《战国策·秦策》作"征敌伐国。"应适莫如后者，后起者常得天下，故应敌莫如后也。《老子》第67章："我有三宝，持而保之：一曰慈，二曰俭，三曰不敢为天下先。……不敢为天下先，故能成器长。"

【译文】

所谓德，就是率先施德于民的意思。所以施德于民越早越好，而与敌人交战还是后发制人的好。

天不变其常，地不易其则

The law of heaven will never change; the earth prospers under its rule.

天不变其常，地不易其则，春秋
冬夏不更其节，古今一也。

《管子·形势》

The law of heaven will never change; the earth prospers under its rule; under it the four seasons have their own natural phenomena; this has been a natural law unchanged since ancient times.

【注释】

常：法典。《管子·幼官》："明法审数，立常备能，则治。"《管子·形势解》："天覆万物，制寒暑，行日月，次星辰，天之常也。""用常者治，失常者乱，天未尝变其所以治也。故曰：天不变其常。"则：法则。《诗经·大雅·烝民》："天生烝民，有物有则。"《管子·形势解》："地生养万物，地之则也。""用则者安，不用则者危，地未尝易其所以安也。故曰：地不易其则。"春秋冬夏：《管子·形势解》："春者阳气始上，故万物生。夏者阳气毕上，故万物长。秋者阴气始下，故万物收。冬者阴气毕下，故万物藏。故春夏生长，秋冬收藏，四时之节也。"

【译文】

天不改变它的常规，地不改变它的法则，四季不改变它的节令，自古至今，始终不变。

天道之极，远者自亲

Strangers will establish harmony among themselves if the law of nature is followed well.

天道之极，远者自亲；人事之起，近亲造怨。

《管子·形势》

Strangers will establish harmony among themselves if the law of nature is followed well; even intimates will hold a grudge against each other if the idea for pursuing the personal interests occurs to them.

【注释】

"行天道，出公理，则远者自亲。废天道，行私为，则子母相怨。"（《管子·形势解》）**天道**：自然的规律。《荀子·天伦》："天有常道矣，地有常数矣。"汉·王充《论衡·乱龙》："鲸鱼死，慧星出，天道自然，非人事也。"古人认为天道是支配人类命运的天神意志。唐·房玄龄《管子》注："天道平分，远近无二，故远者自亲也。"**人事**：人世上人与人之间的各种事情。唐·房玄龄《管子》注："人事则爱恶相攻，故有近亲造怨也。"《史记·太史公自序》："夫《春秋》，上明三王之道，下辨人事之纪。"唐·杜甫《小至》："天时人事日相催，冬至阳生春又来。"

【译文】

完全按自然规律办事，疏远的人也会亲近；人与人之间私心杂念一旦萌生，即使亲近的人也会生怨。

天时不祥，则有水旱

When the meteorological pattern is irregular, floods and droughts occur.

天时不祥，则有水旱；地道不宜，则有饥馑；人道不顺，则有祸乱。

《管子·五辅》

When the meteorological pattern is irregular, floods and droughts occur. When the condition of the earth is unfit, poor harvests and famines befall. When moral standards are decadent, calamities and scourges arise.

【注释】

天时：农时。《荀子·王霸》：“农夫朴力而寡能，则上不失天时，下不失地利，中得人和而百事不废。”也指天道，一般指天文气象等方面的自然现象和规律。祥：吉利。《礼记·礼运》：“嘏以慈告，是谓大祥。”地道：关于地面的自然现象及规律。《管子·霸言》：“立政出令用人道，施爵禄用地道，举大事用天道。”《易·说卦》：“立地之道曰柔与刚。”柔和刚是地道的两个方面。《中庸》引孔子语曰：“人道敏政，地道敏树”，朱熹注：“敏，速也。”指草木生长。人道：人类社会的道德规范。《易·说卦》：“立人之道曰仁与义。”《礼记·丧服小礼》：“亲亲、尊尊、长长、男女之有别，人道之大者也。”鲁哀公问孔子：“人道什么为大？”孔子曰：“人道政为大。”（《礼记·哀公问》）

【译文】

天时不吉祥，就会有水旱之灾；地利不适宜，庄稼无收就会有饥荒发生；人道不和顺，就会发生祸乱。

天下不患无臣，患无君以使之

There is no lack of capable officials, just the want of a monarch to make good use of them.

天下不患无臣，患无君以使之。
天下不患无财，患无人以分之。

《管子·牧民》

There is no lack of capable officials, just the want of a monarch to make good use of them. There is no lack of money, just the want of a virtuous man to manage it.

【注释】

管子曰："故知时者可立以为长，无私者可置以为政，审于时而察于用而能备官者，可奉以为君也。"**患**：忧虑。《论语·季氏》："不患寡而患不均。"**臣**：君主时代的官吏。《礼记·礼运》："故仕于公曰臣。"《仪礼·士丧礼》："乃赴于君。"郑玄注："臣，君之股肱耳目。"

【译文】

天下不愁没有能做官的人，只愁没有明君来差使他们。天下不愁没有财富，只愁没有人来管理财富。

天下无私爱也，无私憎也

The rule of nature is just and disinterested, without partiality and prejudice.

天下无私爱也，无私憎也，为善者有福，为不善者有祸。祸福在为，故先王重为。

《管子·枢言》

The rule of nature is just and disinterested, without partiality and prejudice. Good shall be rewarded with good, and evil with evil. Therefore, the late emperor emphasized good deeds.

【注释】

私爱：偏爱。为：作，行为，担当。《尚书·益稷》："予欲宣力四方，汝为。"《论语·颜渊》："子曰：'为之难，言之得无讱乎'？"知道做起来不容易，说话能不谨慎吗？

【译文】

天道公正无私没有偏爱，也没有偏恶，行善得福，行恶得祸，祸福在于行善或行恶，所以先王看重行为。

天下者，无常乱，无常治

The land under heaven will never be in constant chaos or in everlasting order.

管子说

天下者，无常乱，无常治。不善人在则乱，善人在则治，在于既善所以感之也。

《管子·小称》

The land under heaven will never be in constant chaos or in everlasting order. When an immoral monarch reins, turmoil arises. When a moral leader rules, order is secured. The land under heaven will remain peaceful and stable because of the good will and good deeds that influence and reform the people.

【注释】

治：与"乱"相对。特指政治清明安定。《易·系辞下》："黄帝尧舜垂衣裳而天下治。"善人：有道德的人。《论语·述而》："善人，吾不得而见之矣；得见有恒者，斯可矣。"在于既善所以感之也：注曰："既，尽也。天下所以理，在于君人者内外尽善感之于人也。"

【译文】

天下形势不会一直混乱，也不会一直清明安定。无德之人主政，天下就混乱，有德之人主政，天下就清明安定。天下所以安定，是因为执政者的内外皆善的行为感化了百姓。

听之术，曰：勿望而距，勿望
而许

The way to take advice is to examine it after listening to someone; one should not accept or reject it hastily.

听之术，曰：勿望而距，勿望而许。许之则失守，距之则闭塞。

《管子·九守》

The way to take advice is to examine it after listening to someone; one should not accept or reject it hastily. A person's principles will be violated if they accept advice blindly; however, no one will give advice to one who readily ignores other's opinions.

【注释】

唐·房玄龄注曰："听言之术，必须审察，不可望风则有所距，有所许也。""既未审察，辄有距而许之，故或失守，或闭塞。"勿望而距：不要望风而拒绝。距，拒绝，通"拒"。许：应允，认可。《孟子·梁惠王上》："明足以察秋毫之末而不见舆薪，则王许之乎？"失守：丧失平日坚守的原则。《管子·七臣七主》："法令者，君臣之所共立也；权势者，人主之所独守也。故人主失守则危，臣吏失守则乱。"

【译文】

听取意见的方法就是，听后必须审察，不可望风而拒绝或应允。盲目应允就会失去原则，盲目拒绝就会阻塞言路。

万物之于人也，无私近也，无私远也

Nothing in the world is in shortage or in abundance.

万物之于人也，无私近也，无私远也，巧者有余，而拙者不足。

《管子·形势》

Nothing in the world is in shortage or in abundance. A skilful person can find a thing in abundance while an inept man finds it in shortage.

【注释】

万物之于人也，无私近也，无私远也：唐·房玄龄注："动物则有识而无知，植物则有生而无识，故于人也，无私远近。"私，偏爱。《仪礼·燕礼》："寡君，君之私也。"巧者有余，而拙者不足："古者武王地方不过百里，战卒之众不过万人，然能战胜攻取，立为天子，而世谓之圣王者，知为之之术也。桀、纣贵为天子，富有海内，地方甚大，战卒甚众，而身死国亡，为天下僇者，不知为之之术也。故能为之，则小可为大，贱可为贵。不能为之，则虽为天子，人犹存之也。故曰：巧者有余，而拙者不足。"（《管子·形势解》）巧，灵巧。《周礼·考工记》："材有美，工有巧。"拙，笨。与"巧"相对。

【译文】

天下万物对于人都是公平的，无远无近，巧者用之有余，拙者用之不足。

为人君者中正而无私，为人臣者
忠信而不党

The monarch should be upright and unselfish, an official honest and fair-minded.

为人君者中正而无私，为人臣者忠信而不党，为人父者慈惠以教，为人子者孝悌以肃，为人兄者宽裕以诲，为人弟者比顺以敬，为人夫者敦懞以固，为人妻者劝勉以贞。

《管子·五辅》

The monarch should be upright and unselfish, an official honest and fair-minded, a father benign and instructive, a son filial to his parents, an elder brother generous and tolerant, a younger brother respectful and obedient; the husband should be kind and sincere in order to strengthen his marriage, while the wife should be diligent and faithful.

【注释】

中正：正直。《管子·五辅》："其君子上中正而下谄谀，其士民贵武勇而贱得利。" **忠信**：诚恳，实在。**党**：阿附，偏私。《尚书·洪范》："无偏无党，王道荡荡。" **慈惠**：慈爱，优惠。《管子·势第》："故贤者诚信以仁之，慈惠以爱之。" **孝悌**：孝顺父母，敬爱兄长。**肃**：恭敬。《汉书·五行志》："貌之不恭，是谓不肃。" **宽裕**：宽容。**比顺**：和顺。**敦懞**：惇厚，朴实。《管子·五辅》："敦懞纯固，以备祸乱。" **固**：稳固，使巩固。**贞**：封建社会多指妇女守节。

【译文】

为君主者正直而无私，为臣下者诚实而不阿附，为人父者对子女慈爱教育，为人子者孝敬父母，做兄长要宽厚，做弟弟要敬爱和顺，做丈夫要惇厚朴实以巩固夫妻感情，做妻子要勤勉对丈夫忠贞。

我有善则立誉我，我有过则立毁我

I was acclaimed after I committed an act of beneficence, and condemned soon after I committed an act of
malevolence.

我有善则立誉我，我有过则立毁我。当民之毁誉也，则莫归问于家矣。

《管子·小称》

I was acclaimed after I committed an act of beneficence, and condemned soon after I committed an act of malevolence. I can judge my reputation by the response of the people; there is no need to ask my intimates for their judgements.

【注释】

管子曰："民之观也察矣，不可遁逃。"注曰："有过必知，故不可以遁逃。"立：即刻，马上。**毁誉**：毁谤或称誉。毁，毁谤。《论语·卫灵公》："吾之于人也，谁毁谁誉。"誉，称人之美。**莫归问于家**：注曰："人既毁誉，则己之善恶审矣，故不复问家。问家，则左右佞媚者，善掩其过，而饰其非也。"张文虎注："'莫归问于家'，言善与过，视民之誉毁，不必问之家人。"

【译文】

我做得好可以随时称赞我，我有错可以马上指责我。只看百姓对我是毁是誉就可以了，不必再问自家人。

乌集之交，初虽相驩，后必相咄

Relations developed in a motley crowd may be intimate at first, but will finally cease to exist.

乌集之交，初虽相驩，后必相
咄。故曰：乌集之交，虽善不亲。

《管子·形势解》

Relations developed in a motley crowd may be intimate at first, but will finally cease to exist. Crows that flock together may seem close but will never form long friendship.

【注释】

管子曰："与人交，多诈伪，无情实，偷取一切，谓之乌集之交。" **乌集之交**：如乌鸦集散之交往。《汉书·五行志》："乌集醉饱吏民之家。"颜师古注："乍合乍离，如乌之集。"乌鸦之性好猜，初虽相善，后终不亲。**驩**（huān），同"欢"。《史记·蔺相如传》："且以一璧之故，逆强秦之驩，不可！" **咄**（duō），呵斥。

【译文】

像乌鸦聚集一样的交往，开始虽也亲密，终必离散。所以说：乌集之交，看起来虽然友好但并不亲密。

无土而欲富者忧，无德而欲王
者危

A man who has no land, yet wants to be rich, is
sad; a man who has no virtue, yet wants to be king, is
dangerous.

无土而欲富者忧，无德而欲王者危，施薄而求厚者孤。

《管子·霸言》

A man who has no land, yet wants to be rich, is sad; a man who has no virtue, yet wants to be king, is dangerous; a man who has little commitment, yet wants to be rewarded, is lonely and helpless.

【注释】

无土而欲富者忧：注曰："无土欲富，犹缘木而求鱼，故忧。"土，土地。土生五谷，中国古代以农业为本，无土地欲富是无本之木，无源之水。**无德而欲王者危**：注曰："无德而王，犹欲进而却行，故危。"**施薄而求厚者孤**：注曰："施薄求厚，人必不应，故孤。"施薄求厚，施恩惠于人的少，而求人回报的多。

【译文】

没有土地而想富裕的人会忧愁，无德却想称霸天下的人是危险的，给予人的少而求人回报多的人只会孤独无助。

贤人不至谓之蔽，忠臣不用谓之塞

The capable man is absent because there is someone to dissuade him, the loyal official is ignored because there are obstructions.

贤人不至谓之蔽，忠臣不用谓之塞，令而不行谓之障，禁而不止谓之逆。

《管子·法法》

The capable man is absent because there is someone to dissuade him, the loyal official is ignored because there are obstructions, the issued decree is not enforced because it meets blockades, the ban doesn't work because the people reject it.

【注释】

管子曰："蔽塞障逆之君者，不敢杜其门而守其户也，为贤者之不至，令之不行也。"**贤人不至谓之蔽**：黎翔凤案："贤人不至，为有人蔽之。"蔽，遮挡。《史记·项羽纪》："项伯亦拔剑起舞，常以身翼蔽沛公。"**忠臣不用谓之塞**：忠，忠诚。《荀子·大略》："比干子胥忠而君不用。"塞，堵，阻隔。《墨子·亲士》："谄谀在侧，善议障塞，则国危矣。"**障**：阻隔。**逆**：拒。《国语·晋语》："翟人出逆。"

【译文】

有才能的人不来是有人遮挡，忠臣不受重用是有堵塞，政令下达却不能顺利执行是有阻隔，禁而不止叫做抗拒。

宪律制度必法道，号令必著明，
赏罚必信密

Laws and regulations must follow the principles of the Tao; orders must be clear; rewards and punishments must be appropriate.

宪律制度必法道，号令必著明，赏罚必信密，此王民之经也。

《管子·法法》

Laws and regulations must follow the principles of the Tao; orders must be clear; rewards and punishments must be appropriate; all these are the right methods to govern the people.

【注释】

宪律：法令，法律。宪，法令。《管子·立政》："宪既布，有不行宪者，谓之不从令，罪死不赦。"律，法律。《易·师》："师出以律。"法：效法，遵守。《易·系辞上》："崇效天，卑法地。"著：明显，显露。《礼记·中庸》："诚则形，形则著，著则明。"信密：处理得当。密，一作"必"。《管子·版法解》："刑赏信必，则善劝而奸止。"

【译文】

法令制度一定要遵循道的原则，号令一定要显明，赏罚一定要得当，这是统治百姓的正确方法。

小谨者不大立, 訾食者不肥体

An overcautious person seldom has lofty aspirations, as and a man suffering from anorexia cannot gain weight.

小谨者不大立，訾食者不肥体。

《管子·形势》

An overcautious person seldom has lofty aspirations, as a man suffering from anorexia cannot gain weight.

【注释】

谨：谨慎。《尚书·盘庚上》："恪谨天命。"《管子·形势解》："谨于一家则立于一家，谨于一乡则立于一乡，谨于一国则立于一国，谨于天下则立于天下。是故其所谨者小，则其所立亦小。其所谨者大，则其所立亦大。故曰：小谨者，不大立。"《汉书·郦食其传》："举大事不细谨。"细谨，小谨也。**訾食**：厌食。訾（zǐ），恶。同"龇（cī）"。《管子·形势解》："谏者，所以安主也。食者，所以肥体也。主恶谏则不安，人訾食则不肥。故曰：訾食者，不肥体也。"

【译文】

谨小慎微的人难有大志，好比厌食的人吃不胖一样。

孝弟者，仁之祖也

Filial piety is the origin of benevolence.

孝弟者，仁之祖也。忠信者，交之庆也。

《管子·戒第》

Filial piety is the origin of benevolence, as only a faithful and steadfast person can make a good friend.

【注释】

孝弟者，仁之祖也：注曰："仁从孝弟生，故为仁祖。"孝弟，孝顺父母，敬爱兄长。《论语·学而》："孝弟也者，其为仁之本与。"也作"孝悌"。仁，古代一种含义广泛的道德观念，其核心指人与人相亲，爱人。《论语·雍也》："夫仁者，己欲立而立人，己欲达而达人。"《墨子·经说下》："仁，仁爱也。"**忠信者，交之庆也**：注曰："有忠信之心，故能庆交友之善。"忠信，诚恳实在。《论语·颜渊》："主忠信，徙义，崇德也。"交，结交，往来。《楚辞·九歌·湘君》："交不忠兮怨长，期不信兮告余以不间。"庆，祝贺。《国语·周语中》："晋既克楚于鄢，使郤至告庆于周。"

【译文】

孝敬父母、敬爱兄长是仁爱的根本，诚恳实在，才能交到好朋友。

邪莫如蚤禁之

It is better to put an end to evil thoughts and deeds in their gestational period.

邪莫如蚤禁之。赦过遗善，则民不励。有过不赦，有善不积，励民之道，于此乎用之矣。

《管子·法法》

It is better to put an end to evil thoughts and deeds in their gestational period. Pardoning a crime yet ignoring good deeds will prevent the people from working hard. Not pardoning minor crimes while rewarding small acts of goodness is the right way to encourage the people.

【注释】

邪莫如蚤禁：歪门邪道不如早禁止。邪（xié），不正。《尚书·大禹谟》："任贤勿贰，去邪勿疑。"蚤，同"早"。**赦过**：施恩惠放免罪过。**善**：惠。**励**：勤勉。通"厉"。《国语·吴语》："请王励士，以奋其朋势。"**有善不积**：有小善就赏之，不等到积成大善再赏，故曰"有善不积"。

【译文】

歪门邪道不如早禁止。放免罪过和对善行不加褒扬，百姓就不会勤勉努力。罪小不赦免，善小必有赏，这才是勉励百姓的正道，在这里正用上。

邪行亡乎体，违言不存口，静然
定生，圣也

The man who leads a peaceful life, free of desires, and without committing or uttering improper deeds and words, is a saint.

邪行亡乎体，违言不存口，静然定生，圣也。

《管子·戒第》

The man who leads a peaceful life, free of desires, and without committing or uttering improper deeds and words, is a saint.

【注释】

邪行亡乎体，违言不存口：注曰："体无邪行，口言必顺。"邪行，不正的行为。亡，无。违言，不顺的话。**静然定生，圣也**：注曰："欲静则生定，如此者圣也。"静，静止。《易·坤·文言》："坤至柔而动也刚，至静而德方。"定，安定。《易·家人》："正家而天下定矣。"

【译文】

不做不正当的事，不说不合情理的话，无欲则生命安定，这样的人就是圣人啊。

心有欲者，物过而目不见，声至
而耳不闻也

A greedy man cannot see or hear clearly.

心有欲者，物过而目不见，声至而耳不闻也。故曰：上离其道，下失其事。

《管子·心术上》

A greedy man cannot see or hear clearly. Therefore, if a man's mind is warped, the rest of his body will not function correctly.

【注释】

管子曰："心之在体，君之位也。九窍之有职，官之分也。耳目者，视听之官也。"**物**：存在于天地间的万物。《诗经·大雅·烝民》："天生烝民，有物有则。"**上离其道，下失其事**：心有贪欲，其他器官不能主事。上，指心。心之官主思，其道当无欲。下，指九窍中其他器官。耳主听，目主视，皆听命于心。故说上离其道，下失其事。

【译文】

心有贪欲，就会万物在眼前却看不见，声音在耳边却听不见。所以说：心一旦离开正道，其他器官就不能主事了。

信之者仁也，不可欺者智也

Honesty and credit are benevolence. And a wise man will not be cheated.

管子说

信之者仁也，不可欺者智也。既智且仁，是谓成人。

《管子·枢言》

Honesty and credit are benevolence. And a wise man will not be cheated. If a man is wise, as well as creditable, he can be said to be the perfect man.

【注释】

信：诚实，不欺。《论语·学而》："与朋友交而不信乎？"仁：人与人相亲，爱人是仁的核心。《论语·雍也》："夫仁者，己欲立而立人，己欲达而达人。"《墨子·经说下》："仁，仁爱也。"智：智慧。成人：德才兼备的人，完人。《论语·宪问》："子路问成人。子曰：'若臧武仲之知，公绰之不欲，卞庄子之勇，冉求之艺，文之以礼乐，亦可以为成人矣。'"

【译文】

诚信就是仁，不受欺骗就是有智慧。如果能做到既有智慧又诚信，也就算是个完人了。

刑罚不足以畏其意

Punishments cannot change the will of the common people.

刑罚不足以畏其意，杀戮不足以服其心。

《管子·牧民》

Punishments cannot change the will of the common people, and executions will not lead to gaining superiority over them either.

【注释】

管子曰："故刑罚繁而意不恐，则令不行矣。杀戮众而心不服，则上位危矣。"畏：通"威"。《韩非子·主道》："其行罚也，畏乎如雷霆，神圣不能解也。"意：愿望，意图。《管子·君臣下》："明君在上，便辟不能食其意。"屈原《楚辞·卜居》："用君之心，行君之意。"服：佩服。也用指制服、征服。《孟子·公孙丑上》："以力服人者，非心服也，力不赡也。"

【译文】

刑罚不能改变百姓的意愿，杀戮也不能使百姓心服。

形不正者德不来

A person with a wretched appearance must be evil inside.

形不正者德不来，中不精者心不治。

《管子·心术下》

A person with a wretched appearance must be evil inside; without honesty and sincerity, one's mind could not be in peace.

【注释】

形不正者德不来：注曰："有诸内必形于外，故德来居中，外形自正。《诗》云：'抑抑威仪，惟德之隅'。"外形不正内必无德，内有德外形自正。中不精者心不治：注曰："精，诚至之谓也。中能诚至，心事自理。"

【译文】

外形不端正，内心一定没有德行，内心不真诚就不会安定。

言是而不能立，言非而不能废

If the good person is cast aside while the evil one stays in office . . .

言是而不能立，言非而不能废，有功而不能赏，有罪而不能诛，若是而能治民者，未之有也。

《管子·七法》

The good person is cast aside while the evil one stays in office; those who render good services are not rewarded, whereas criminals are immune to punishment; such a way of governing the people has been never seen.

【法释】

管子曰："是必立，非必废，有功必赏，有罪必诛，若是安治矣，未也。是何也？曰：形势器械未具，犹之不治也。"意谓仅"立是、废非、赏功、诛罪"还是不够的，还要同时具备"形势器械"的条件才能"治民"。**言是而不能立，言非而不能废**：注曰："谓之是，不能立其人而用之。谓之非，不能废其人而退之。"

【译文】

对好人不能任用，对坏人不能废退，对有功者不能赏，对有罪者不能罚，这样能统治百姓，是没有的事。

一年之计，莫如树谷

When planning for a year, plant cereals.

一年之计，莫如树谷；十年之计，莫如树木；终身之计，莫如树人。

《管子·权修》

When planning for a year, plant cereals. When planning for a decade, plant trees. When planning for life, train and educate the people.

【注释】

管子曰："一树一获者，谷也。一树十获者，木也。一树百获者，人也。"获（huò），收割，收成。《诗经·豳风·七月》："八月其获。"又"十月获稻"。《国语·吴语》："以岁之不获也，无有诛焉。"**树谷**：栽种五谷。树，种，植。《诗经·小雅·巧言》："荏染柔木，君子树之。"《淮南子·原道》："夫萍树根于水，木树根于土。"**树人**：培植人才。《管子》注："树人，谓济而成立之。""人有百年之寿。虽使无百年，子孙亦有嗣之而报德者，故曰百获也。"

【译文】

为一年算计，不如种植五谷；为十年算计，不如种植树木；为一辈子算计，不如培养人才。

一期之师，十年之蓄积弹

A troop of soldiers fighting a war will cost ten years of national savings.

一期之师，十年之蓄积殚。一战之费，累代之功尽。

《管子·参患》

A troop of soldiers fighting a war will cost ten years of national savings; a nation fighting a war will have the cost of ruining the merits and achievements made by several generations.

【注释】

一期：一次会战。期，会。屈原《离骚》："路不周以左转兮，指西海以为期。" 殚（dān）：尽。《孙子·作战》："力屈财殚。" 一战之费，累代之功尽：注曰："倾国一战，能尽累代之功。"功，劳绩。《周礼·夏官·司勋》："王功曰勋，国功曰功。"

【译文】

军队打一次仗，能耗费国家十年积蓄。举国一战，能耗尽几代人的功绩。

有善者不留其赏，故民不私其利

If good conduct is rewarded immediately, the people will not pursue personal interests.

有善者不留其赏，故民不私其利。有过者不宿其罚，故民不疾其威。

《管子·君臣上》

If good conduct is rewarded immediately, the people will not pursue personal interests. If wrong deeds are punished without delay, the people will not complain about the severity of the penalties.

【注释】

有善者不留其赏：有善必赏。留，稽留，迟滞。《易·旅》："君子以明慎用刑，而不留狱。" 私其利：注曰："善必得赏，私利何为？" 私利，犹言一己之利益。《管子·禁藏》："民多私利者，其国贫。" 有过者不宿其罚，故民不疾其威：唐·房玄龄注曰"罚得其过，则人不疾其威。疾，怨也。" 宿，隔夜。威，权势。《韩非子·诡使》："威者所以行令也。"

【译文】

有善行及时行赏，所以百姓不会心怀私利。有过错及时惩罚，所以百姓不会抱怨执法威严。

欲王天下而失天之道，天下不可
得而王也

To unite the land of heaven without following the laws of heaven is impossible.

欲王天下而失天之道，天下不可得而王也。得天之道，其事若自然；失天之道，虽立不安。

《管子·形势》

To unite the land of heaven without following the laws of heaven is impossible. Following these laws, unification will naturally occur; ignoring them, peace will not be secured even though unification is achieved.

【注释】

自然：天然，非人为的。《老子》第 25 章："人法地，地法天，天法道，道法自然。"宋·王安石《老子》："本者，出之自然，故不假乎人之力而万物以生也。"

【译文】

想统一天下却不用天道，天下是没法统一的。用天道，统一天下是自然而然的事；不用天道，即使统一了天下也不会安定。

早知敌而独行，有蓄积则久而
不匮

There is no war that cannot be won if an army knows much about its enemy in advance; it will not be exhausted because financial and material supply is guaranteed.

早知敌而独行，有蓄积则久而不匮，器械巧则伐而不费，赏罚明则勇士劝也。

《管子·兵法》

There is no war that cannot be won if an army knows much about its enemy in advance; it will not be exhausted because financial and material supply is guaranteed. Fine weapons will accelerate its victory, and clear rewards and punishments will provide the best boost to morale.

【注释】

早知敌：提前掌握敌情。管子曰："兵无主则不早知敌。"注曰："兵无主，则人怀苟且，故不能知敌。"独行：战必胜，守必固，如入无人之境，故曰独行。匮(kuì)：空乏，穷尽。《韩非子·外储说右下》："管仲曰：'臣闻之，上有积财，则民臣必匮乏于天下。'"器械巧：武器精良。管子曰："器械不巧则朝无定。"注曰："器械不巧，则寇敌见凌，故朝无定。"赏罚明：赏功罚过分明。管子曰："赏罚不明则民轻其产。"注曰："赏罚不明，则人无聊生，故轻其产。"产，生也。劝：勉励，奖励。《论语·为政》："举善而教不能则劝。"《左传·成公十四年》："惩恶而劝善。"

【译文】

提前掌握敌情就能战无不胜，财物储备多就能久战而不匮乏，武器精良就能取胜快不浪费时间，赏罚分明就能让战士得到最好的勉励。

朝忘其事，夕失其功

One who has accomplished nothing at the end of the day must not have worked hard during the day.

朝忘其事，夕失其功。邪气袭内，正色乃衰。

《管子·形势》

One who has accomplished nothing at the end of the day must not have worked hard during the day. A man will have a wretched appearance if he is evil and wicked inside.

【注释】

朝忘其事，夕失其功：朝不勉力务进，夕无见功。朝，早晨。《论语·里仁》："朝闻道，夕死可矣。"忘，通"亡"。夕，傍晚。《诗经·王风·君子于役》："日之夕矣，羊牛下来。"**邪气袭内，正色乃衰**：心存不正之气，面现衰容。《管子·形势解》："中情信诚则名誉美矣，修行谨敬则尊显附矣。中无情实则名声恶矣，修行慢易则污辱生矣。故曰：邪气袭内，正气乃衰也。"邪气，不正之气。汉·东方朔《七谏·自悲》："邪气入而感内兮，施玉色而外淫。"正色，表情端庄严肃。《尚书·毕命》："正色率下。"疏："正色，谓严其颜色，不惰慢，不阿谄。"一说"正"当为"玉"。衰，"盛"之对。《论语·微子》："凤兮凤兮，何德之衰。"

【译文】

早晨不勉力务进，晚上就没有成果。不正之气侵入内心，面容就会正气衰退。

召远在修近，闭祸在除怨

If one gets along well with the people around him, those who live afar will wish to go to him for shelter. If resentment is appeased, turmoil will not arise.

召远在修近，闭祸在除怨，修长在乎任贤，安高在乎同利。

《管子·版法》

If one gets along well with the people around him, those who live afar will wish to go to him for shelter. If resentment is appeased, turmoil will not arise. If a monarch governs with capable officials, long-term peace and the stability of the nation will be ensured, and if he is of one mind with the people, his authority will be firm and steady.

【注释】

召远在修近：管子曰："爱施之德，虽行而无私。内行不修，则不能朝远方之君。"注曰："修近则远者至。"**闭祸在除怨**：管子曰："凡祸乱之所生，生于怨咎。怨咎所生，生于非理。"注曰："除怨则祸端塞。"**修长在乎任贤**：管子曰："凡人君所以尊安者，贤佐也。"注曰："任贤则国祚长。"**安高在乎同利**：管子曰："凡人者，莫不欲利而恶害。是故与天下同利者，天下持之；擅天下之利者，天下谋之。"注曰："与下同利则高位安。"

【译文】

与近处的百姓修好，远处的民众就会来投奔，消除怨恨就会不生祸乱，任用有才能的人，国家就能长治久安，能与百姓同享利益，君主才会安泰。

政之所兴，在顺民心

A government decree that meets the aspirations of the common people will be implemented effectively.

政之所兴，在顺民心；政之所废，在逆民心。

《管子·牧民》

A government decree that meets the aspirations of the common people will be implemented effectively; otherwise, it will be of no avail.

【注释】

兴：举。《周礼·夏官·大司马》："进贤兴功，以作邦国。"顺：顺从，顺应。与"逆"相对。《易·革》："小人革面，顺以从君也。"废：废止，停止。《礼记·学记》："此六者，教之所由废也。"《老子》第18章："大道废，有仁义。"《孟子·离娄上》："国之所以废兴存亡者亦然。"逆：不顺。《尚书·太甲下》："有言逆于汝心，必求诸道。"

【译文】

政令通达，在于顺应民心；政令废止，在于不能顺应民心。

治国有三器

There are three instruments—order, weapons, and salary—needed to govern a nation effectively.

治国有三器，乱国有六攻。明君能胜六攻而立三器则国治，不肖之君不能胜六攻而立三器故国不治。

《管子·版法解》

There are three instruments—order, weapons, and salary—needed to govern a nation effectively, and six practices—displaying favoritism, self aggrandizing, being selfish, womanizing, having crafty and fawning behaviors, and an over indulgence in pleasures—that sabotage this effectiveness. A wise and able monarch is able to ban these six practices and install these three instruments, which will govern the state well; while an incompetent monarch will fail to do so which will lead to the disorder of the nation.

【注释】

三器：管子曰："三器者，何也？曰：号令也，斧钺也，禄赏也。""三器之用，何也？曰：非号令无以使下，非斧钺无以畏众，非禄赏无以劝民。"六攻：管子曰："六攻者，何也？亲也，贵也，货也，色也，巧佞也，玩好也。""六攻之败，何也？曰：虽不听而可以得存，虽犯禁而可以得免，虽无功而可以得富。"

【译文】

治理国家有三器，祸乱国家有六攻。英明君主如果能够战胜六攻、用好三器，那么国家就可以大治，败国之主不能战胜六攻、用好三器，国家必乱。

治国之道，必先富民

Enriching the people is the prerequisite to administrate a nation.

治国之道，必先富民，民富则易治也，民贫则难治也。

《管子·治国》

Enriching the people is the prerequisite to administrate a nation; it is easy to establish order if the common people are rich, whereas if they are poor it is a much harder task.

【注释】

管子曰："民富则安乡重家，安乡重家则敬上畏罪，敬上畏罪则易治也。民贫则危乡轻家，危乡轻家则敢陵上犯禁，陵上犯禁则难治也。故治国常富，而乱国必贫。是以善为国者，必先富民，然后治之。"《论语·子路》："子适卫，冉有仆。子曰：'庶矣哉！'冉有曰：'既庶矣，又何加焉？'曰：'富之。'曰：'既富矣，又何加焉？'曰：'教之。'"管子和孔子都主张富民而教。

【译文】

治国之道，必先使百姓富裕，百姓富裕就容易治理，百姓贫穷就难以治理。

众若时雨，寡若飘风

To besiege the enemies and lure them into surrender when overwhelming in number; to launch a surprise attack and triumph over the enemies when few in number.

管子说

众若时雨，寡若飘风，一之终也。

《管子·兵法》

To besiege the enemies and lure them into surrender when overwhelming in number; to launch a surprise attack and triumph over the enemies when few in number; to be able to defeat the enemies under both conditions is the highest achievement of a commander of troops.

【注释】

唐·房玄龄注曰："用众贵详审，故若时雨之渐。用寡贵机速，故若飘风之卒至。此亦以一为本，故能终致此道。"黎翔凤案："我士卒多于敌，则包围诱降而改编之；少于敌，则迅速出奇以制胜。"**众若时雨**：兵力多于敌人时犹如时雨而化之。众，多。《左传·桓公十一年》："师克在和不在众。"时雨，应时之雨。《孟子·梁惠王下》："若时雨降。"**寡若飘风**：兵力少于敌人时以奇兵突袭胜敌。飘风，旋风。《老子》第24章："飘风不终朝，暴雨不终日。"

【译文】

我军数倍于敌时就用包围诱降的办法瓦解他们，我军少于敌人时就用奇兵突袭的战术制服他们。人多能战胜敌人，人少能战胜敌人，这是以道用兵的最高境界。

壮者无怠，老者无偷

Be neither slothful in the meridian of one's life, nor drift along in one's old age.

壮者无怠，老者无偷，顺天之道，必以善终者也。

《管子·中匡》

Be neither slothful in the meridian of one's life, nor drift along in one's old age; by following these laws of nature one will live a full and tranquil life.

【注释】

怠：松懈，懒惰。《尚书·大禹谟》："无怠无荒，四夷来王。"偷：苟且，怠惰。《老子》第41章："建德若偷。"顺天：遵循天道。《左传·文公十五年》："礼以顺天，天之道也。"善终：不遇祸患，终其天年。

【译文】

壮年时不懒惰，老年时不苟且，行事遵循天道，就一定会终享天年的。

追亡逐遁若飘风，击刺若雷电

An army should chase the fleeing enemies as quickly as the wind, and attack the enemies as fiercely as a thunderbolt.

追亡逐遁若飘风，击刺若雷电。绝地不守，恃固不拔。

《管子·兵法》

An army should chase the fleeing enemies as quickly as the wind, and attack the enemies as fiercely as a thunderbolt. Never defend an isolated position, and never launch an attack on an impregnable fortress.

【注释】

追亡逐遁若飘风：追逐溃逃之敌像旋风一样快。遁（dùn），逃走。《左传·庄公二十八年》："楚师夜遁。"飘风，旋风。《诗经·大雅·卷阿》："有卷者阿，飘风自南。"传："飘风，迴风也。"击刺若雷电：攻击敌人如电闪雷鸣一样猛烈。击刺，以剑刺人。绝地：极为险恶而无出路的境地。《孙子·九地》："去国越境而师者，绝地也。"恃固不拔：唐·房玄龄注："拔恃固之守，必多费而无功也。"

【译文】

追逐逃敌像疾风一样快，攻击敌人如万钧雷霆一样猛烈。不据守孤绝之地，不攻打固守之敌。

责任编辑：陆　瑜
英　　译：薛彧威
封面设计：胡　湖
印刷监制：佟汉冬

图书在版编目（CIP）数据

管子说：汉英对照／蔡希勤编注 . —北京：华语
教学出版社，2011
（老人家说系列）
ISBN 978–7–5138–0144–7

Ⅰ.①管… 　Ⅱ.①蔡… 　Ⅲ.①汉语—对外汉语教学—
自学参考资料②法家—汉、英 　Ⅳ.①H195.4②B226.1

中国版本图书馆 CIP 数据核字（2011）第 161628 号

老人家说·管子说

蔡希勤　编注

*

©华语教学出版社
华语教学出版社出版
（中国北京百万庄大街 24 号　邮政编码 100037）
电话：(86)10– 68320585　68997826
传真：(86)10– 68997826　68326333
网址：www.sinolingua.com.cn
电子信箱：hyjx@sinolingua.com.cn
北京市松源印刷有限公司印刷
2012 年（大 32 开）第一版
（汉英）
ISBN 978–7–5138–0144–7
定价：35.00 元